ANIMALS

Learning Experiences for Children

LANGUAGE
ARTS

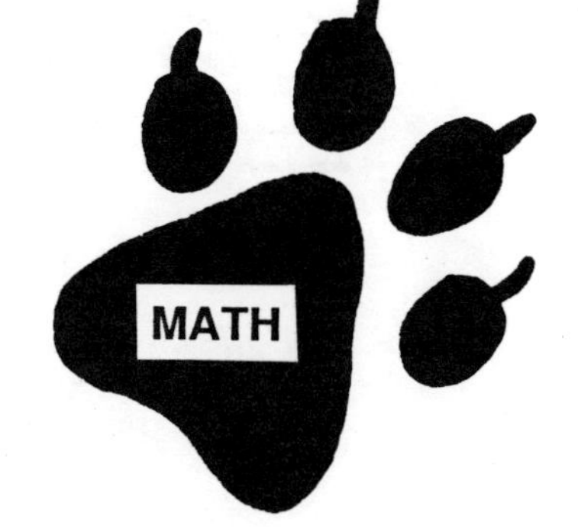

Ann Packard and Shirley Stafford

DALE SEYMOUR PUBLICATIONS

To The Children's School
and to the children,
our loving sources of
creativity and inspiration

Order number DS07712
ISBN 0-86651-382-5
(previously published by the authors under ISBN 0-9607580-5-4)

4 5 6 7 8 9 10 11 12 13-MG-95 94 93 92 91

THIS WE BELIEVE

Education concerns the growth of the whole person. Cognitive, affective, and psychomotor growth are all interrelated, and each plays a vital role in the learning experiences of children. In creating a learning environment that is in harmony with the concept of educating the whole child, we:

- Work toward establishing a safe atmosphere that the child *senses* through the physical environment and *experiences* through personal interactions. There is freedom for children to converse, work together, and move about.
- Strive for the child to have a positive self-image. Each child is a unique individual with specific needs. Each grows and develops at a different rate. There is a trust in the child and a respect for each child's diversity.
- Encourage growth in responsibility, independence, and decision making. The child is an active learner, and each one's creativity is valued.
- Provide a curriculum that is child-centered and subject-centered, taking into account the nature of children as well as the material to be learned.
- View the teacher as a facilitator and a significant person in the life of the child. The teacher's personal and professional growth in needs and responsibilities is recognized.

HOW TO USE THIS BOOK

This book contains:

- *A theme.* The curricular areas are developed within this theme.
- *An integrated curriculum approach.* This approach involves the children simultaneously in the various areas.
- *Open-ended learning experiences appropriate for young children, designed to encourage the creativity of the learner.* Each activity includes a pictorial task card, a statement of purpose, a list of materials needed, directions, and suggestions for extended activities.
- *Bridging devices.* Most of the learning experiences are accompanied by a recording sheet to aid the child's transition from the concrete to the abstract.

This book is categorized for convenience into activities for various types of animals: animals in general, pets, extinct and endangered animals, and teddy bears and other stuffed animals. The activities integrate math, language arts, and cooking. Science and art are also woven throughout the learning experiences.

After introducing the theme of this book (through visual aids, other books, open discussion, music, and dramatic play):

- Develop and integrate the children's ideas into the theme.
- Be alert to your own creativity by expanding or deleting the learning experiences to fit your children's needs.
- Make your graphs, charts, and task cards in the appropriate sizes for your classroom center.
- Provide the sensory materials listed for each experience.
- Duplicate the recording sheets to be used.

THE ACTIVITIES FOR DEVELOPING AN ANIMALS THEME

ANIMALS IN GENERAL

PETS

ENDANGERED AND EXTINCT ANIMALS

TEDDY BEARS AND OTHER STUFFED ANIMALS

LANGUAGE ARTS

Language development is a vital part of the curriculum. The classroom acts as a stimulus for this development. It is crucial to provide opportunities for oral and written language in which children are sharing ideas.

The following learning experiences are designed to interest and involve children in the need to communicate.

MATH

Math helps children think for themselves. The learning experiences here allow children to make their own discoveries as well as introduce them to new possibilities. Manipulation of materials is vital because this gives the children concrete experience with the world of math in place of or prior to abstract recording. Experiences in doing, seeing, using, and exploring are essential in a math curriculum for children.

COOKING

Cooking is naturally suited for instruction in skills and concepts related to various curricular areas.

- *Math:* Children learn how to measure, weigh, divide, sort, classify, count, and estimate.
- *Language:* Cooking encourages language development as the children use new words directly related to what they are actually doing. Cooking is a vocabulary builder that makes abstractions concrete and understandable.
- *Science:* Cooking excites great interest and thus promotes curiosity and inquisitive attitudes toward exploration.
- *Reading:* Cooking requires the skill of reading and makes it purposeful.

ANIMALS IN GENERAL

LEARNING EXPERIENCE: Animal Teams

TASK CARD

Animal Teams

Roll the die.

YELLOW

Even number: Monkeys.
Odd number: Lions.
Fill the grid.

Monkeys	2	6
Lions	5	3

PURPOSE: To provide practice in recognizing odd and even numbers.

MATERIALS AND DIRECTIONS

Dice
Recording Grid
Crayons

Instruction in odd and even numbers should precede this activity. We had the children write the number in the box and then color over it with a light crayon, yellow or orange.

Even 4 6 2 **Animal Teams** 3 1 5 odd

Monkeys								
Lions								

LEARNING EXPERIENCE: Make an Animal Track Book

TASK CARD

Make an animal track book.
Write each animal's name.

PURPOSE: To develop animal track identification skills.

MATERIALS AND DIRECTIONS

Teacher prepares animal track book for each child. Teacher makes up animal track chart. Children refer to chart to complete animal track books.

Brown and black crayons
Pencils

deer
horse
cat
dog
squirrel
bird

Animal Track Book

Name ____________________

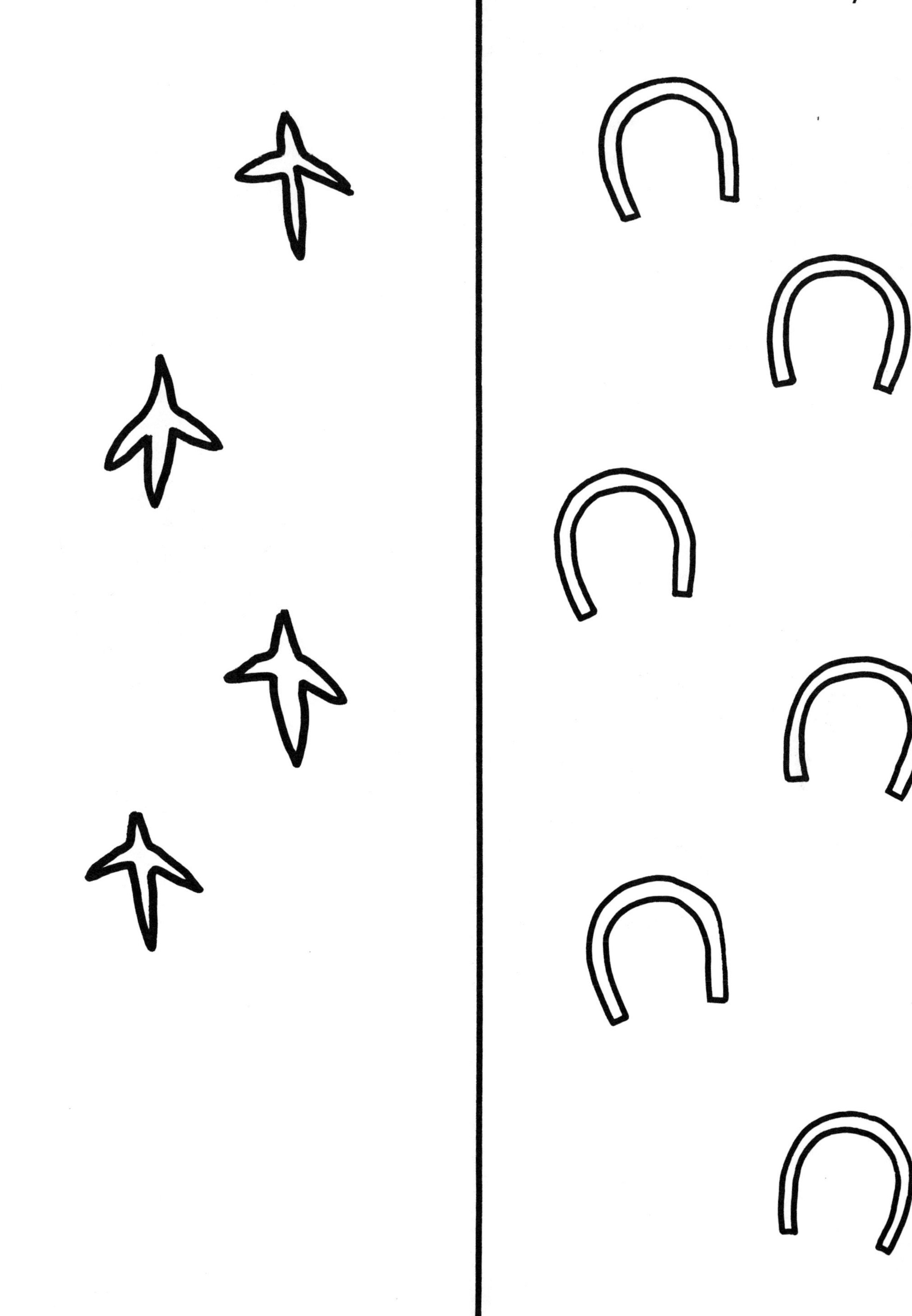

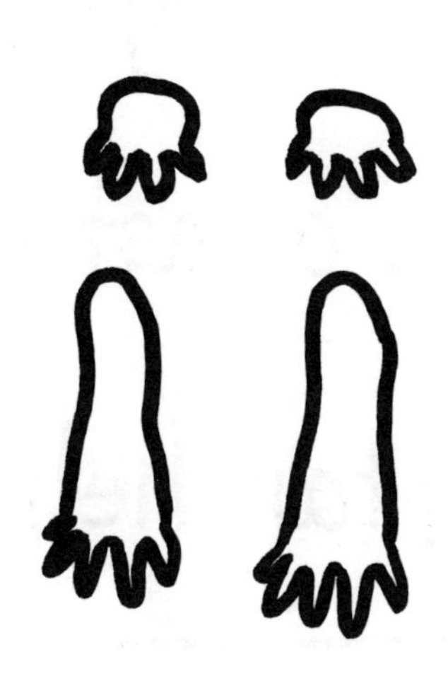

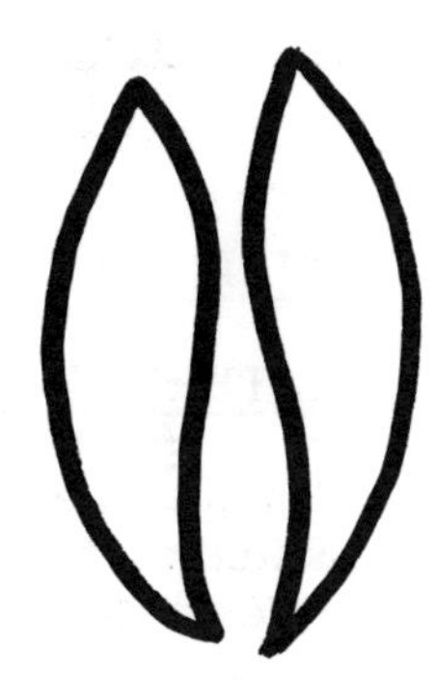

LEARNING EXPERIENCE: Animal Skeletons

TASK CARD

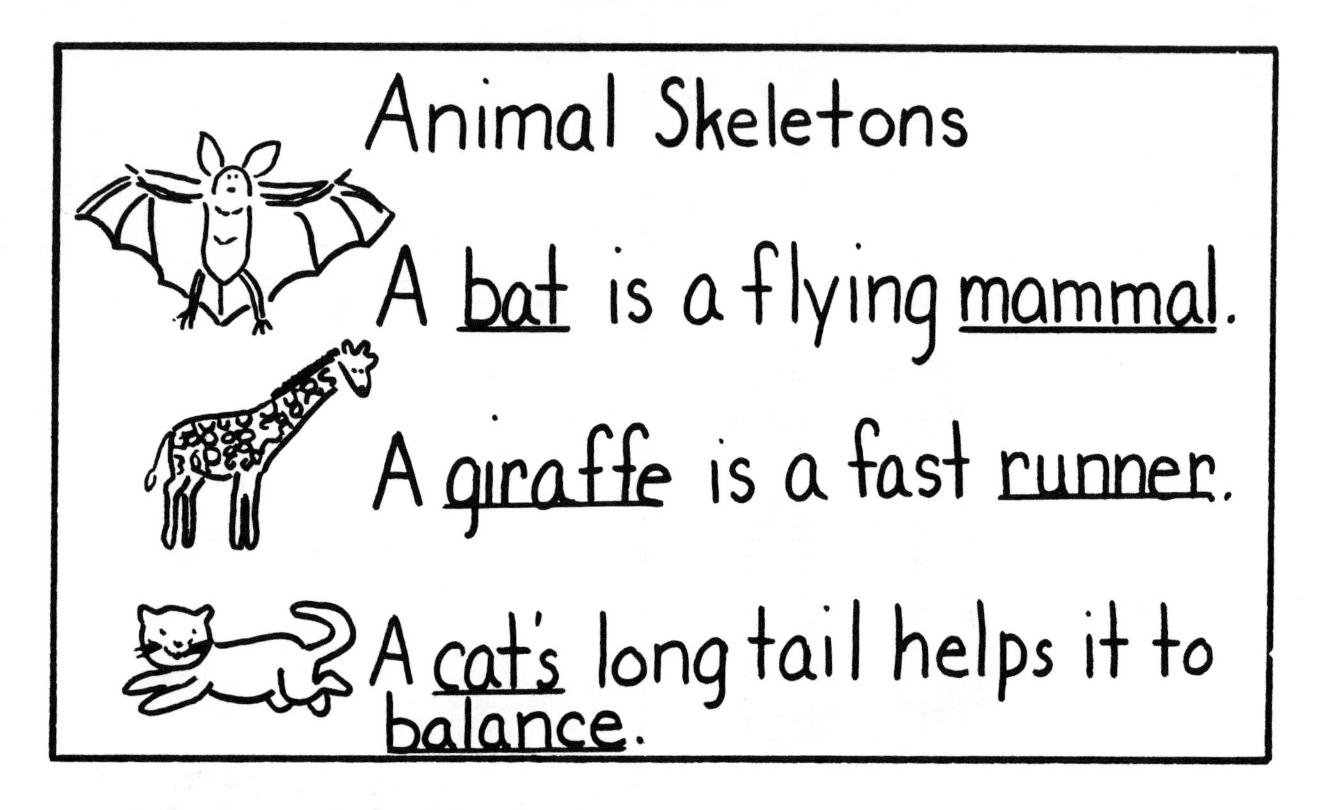

PURPOSE: To familiarize children with animal skeletons.

MATERIALS AND DIRECTIONS

Teacher prepares an animal skeleton book for each child. The child colors the skeletons to look like the living animals. The child fills in the missing words on each page.

Crayons
Pencils

A Look at Animal Skeletons

by ______________________

Giraffe

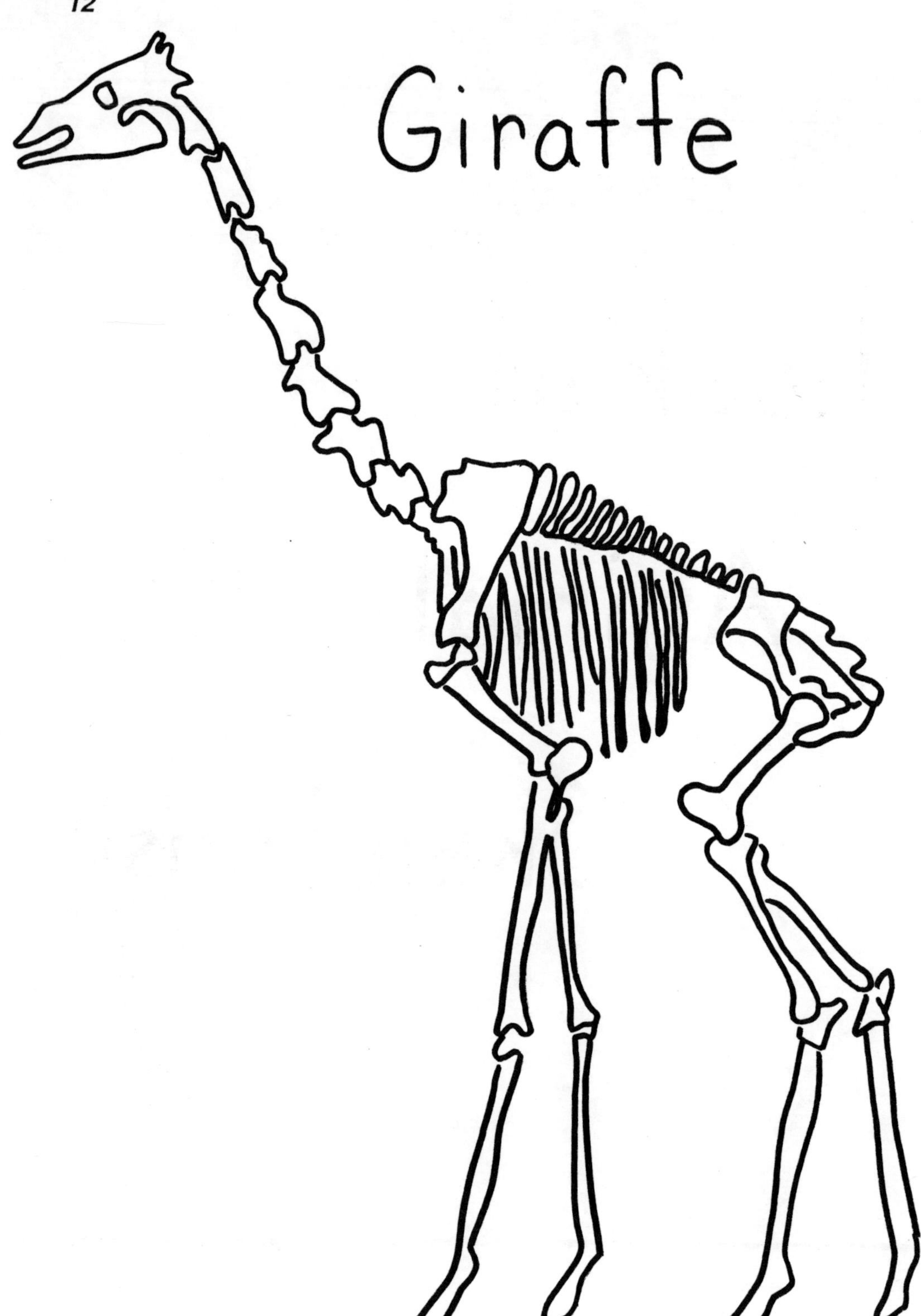

A ________ is a fast ________.
Notice the long leg bones.

Bat

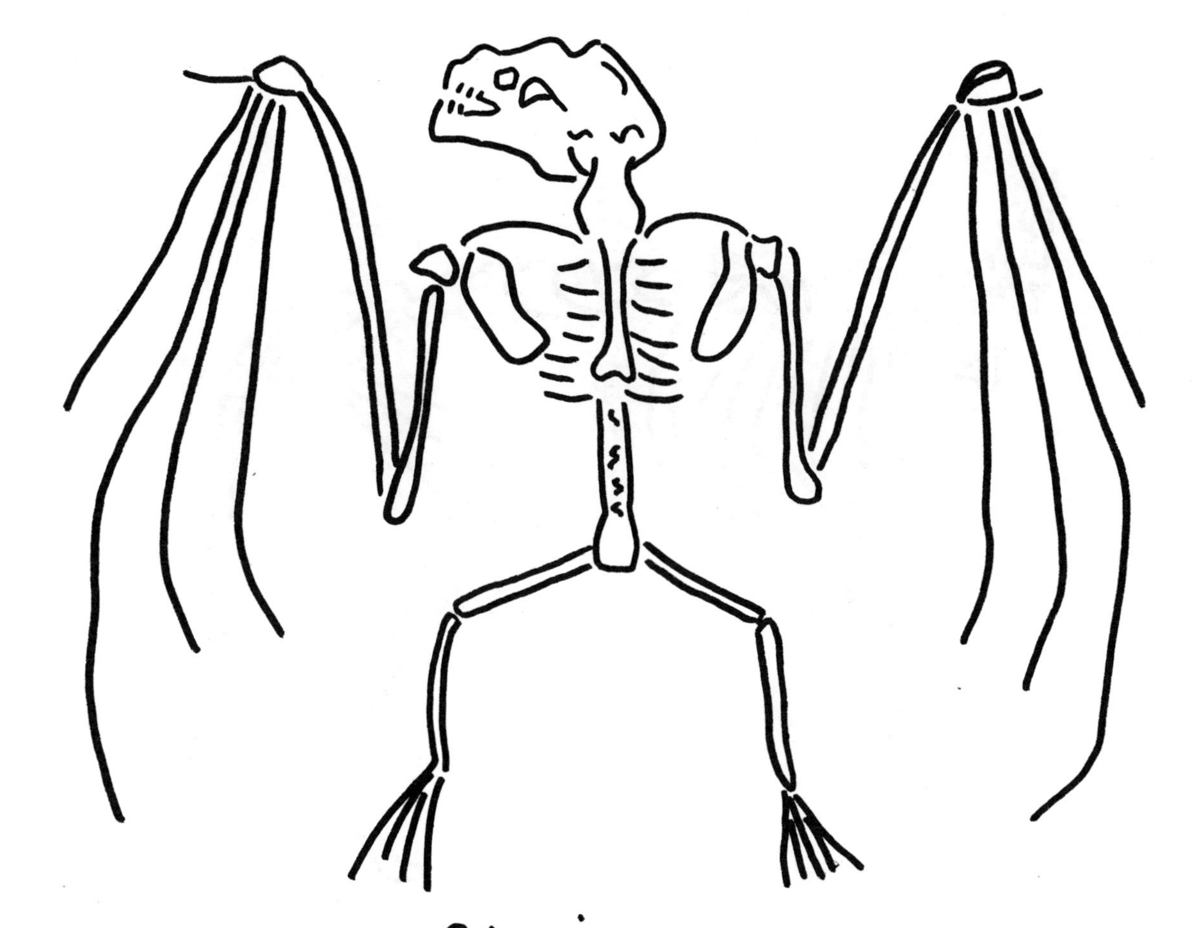

A ____ is a flying __________.
It has light, hollow bones
like a bird.

Cat

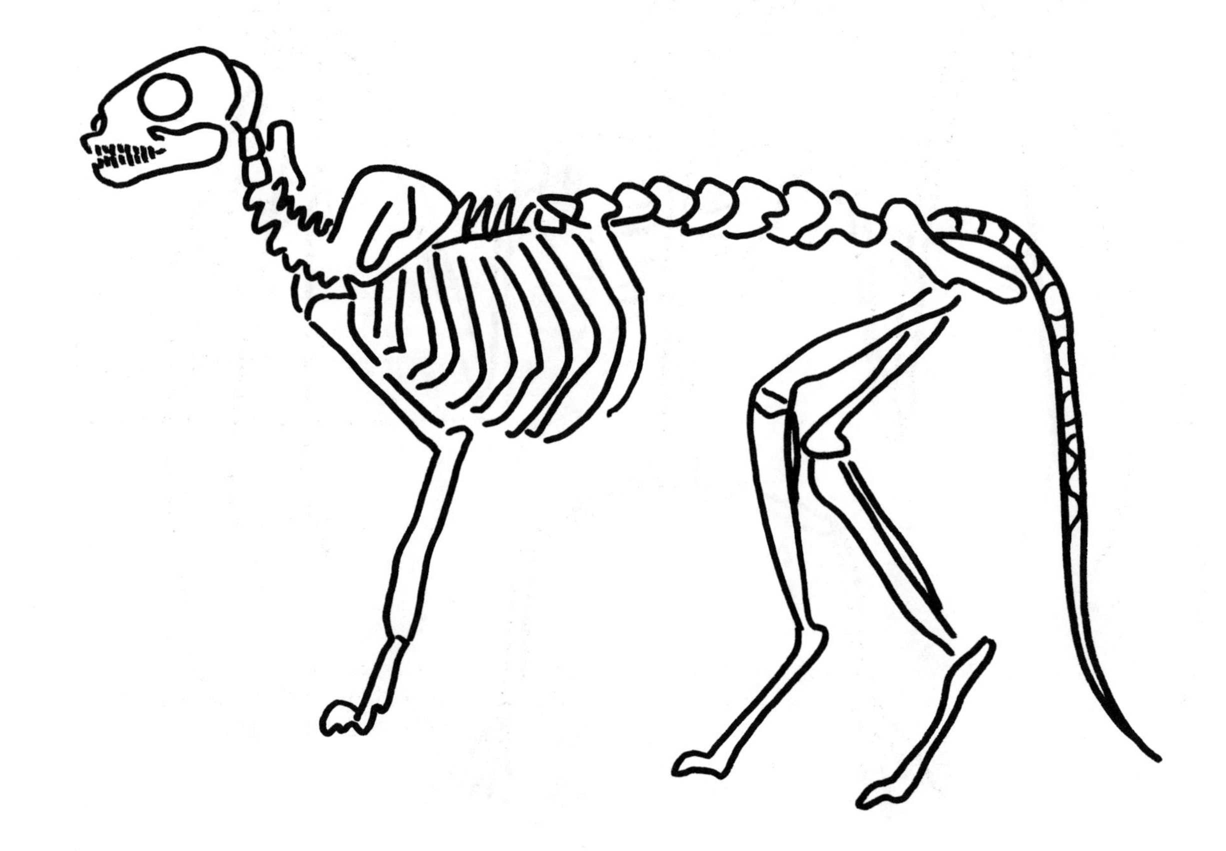

A______long______helps it
to balance when it jumps.

LEARNING EXPERIENCE: Animal Camouflage

TASK CARD

PURPOSE: To define the word 'camouflage'. To explore with the children one adaptation animals use for survival.

MATERIALS AND DIRECTIONS

Teacher runs pages on colored paper: the fish on blue, the underwater scene on blue; the snowy owl on white, the forest scene on white; and the seal and the rocky scene on grey. The child chooses an animal—for example, the seal—cuts it out and glues it on the background.

Glue
Scissors
Felt markers— to add a little color by filling in facial features or outlining animals

Courtesy of Heather McNair, co-teacher with Shirley Stafford.

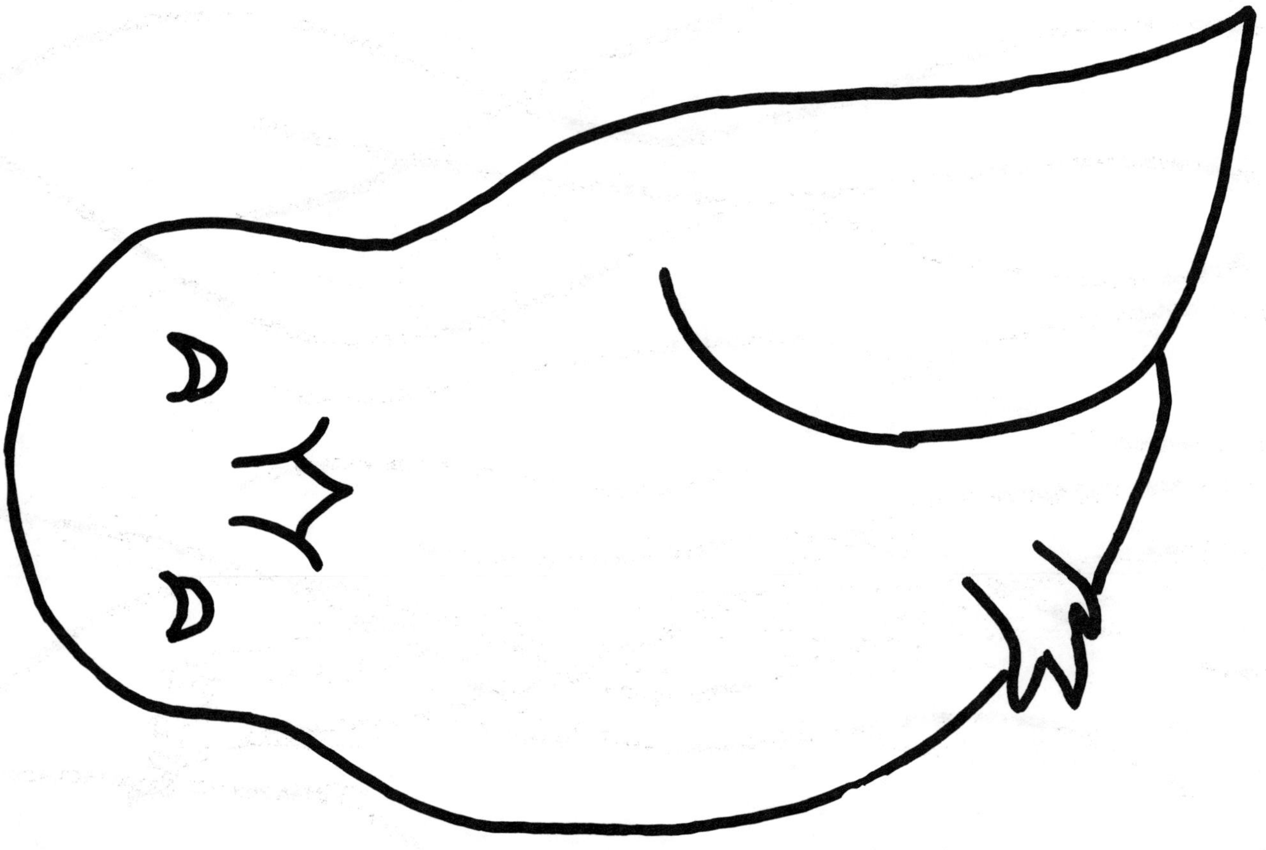

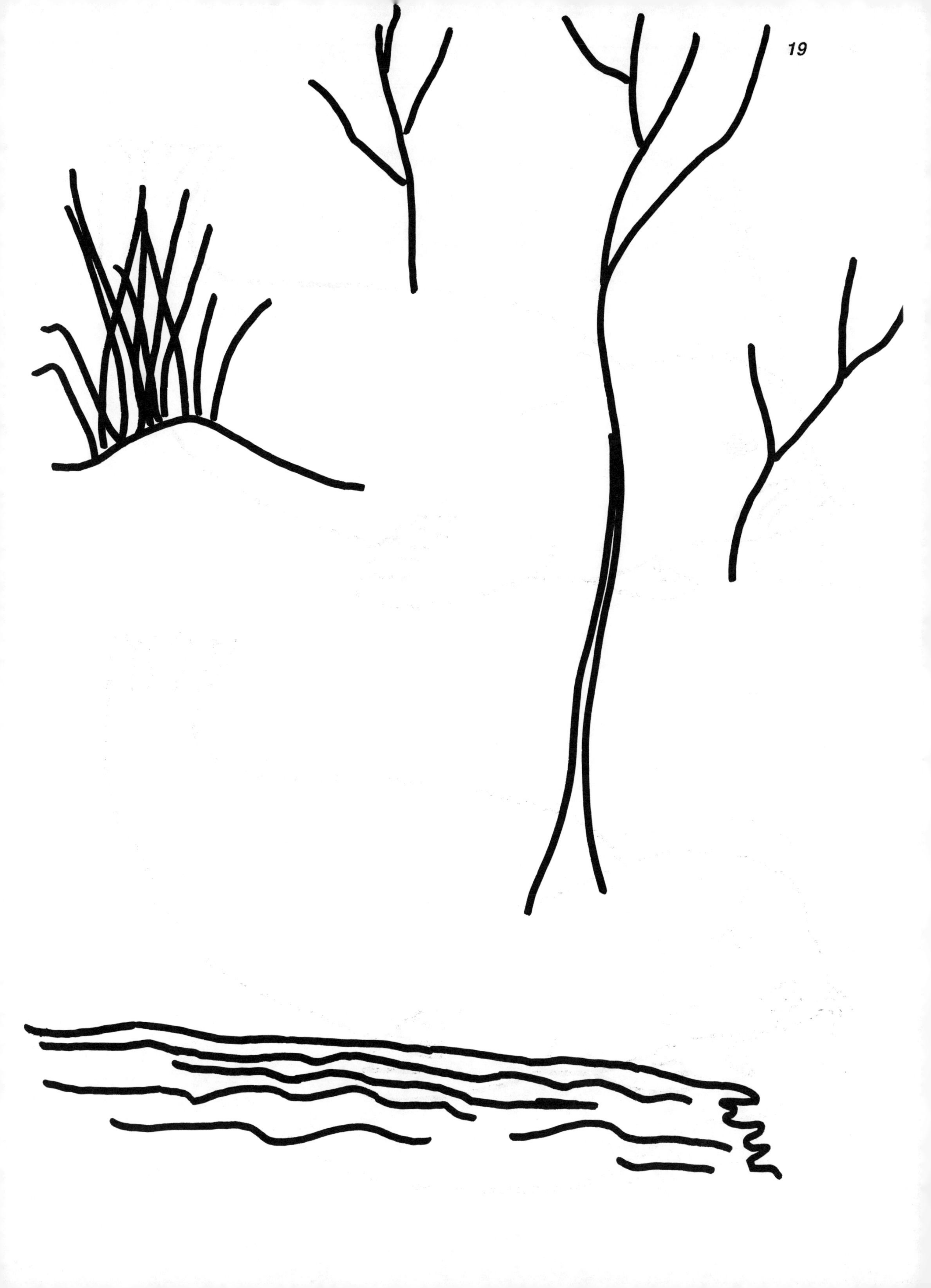

LEARNING EXPERIENCE: Make a Mixed-Up Animal

TASK CARD

PURPOSE: Using animal parts to construct a whole.

MATERIALS AND DIRECTIONS

Teacher provides magazine pictures of animals. Children cut out parts from different animals to construct a mixed-up animal. The children then label the parts.

Glue
Pencils
Scissors

EXTENDED ACTIVITY

* Children often become involved in this activity. To extend it have them make a mixed-up zoo. This can be done by making a cover for a book, titled "Mixed-Up Zoo". The pages in the book will be the pictures of the mixed-up animals. Children like to give their animals funny names so provide a line on each page where they can write the name of each one.

Make a Mixed-up Animal

Label the Parts

Name ______________________________

LEARNING EXPERIENCE: Animal Names

TASK CARD

Animal Names

Think of an animal whose name begins just like yours.

"Shirley Sheep"

Draw a picture, tell a story.

PURPOSE: To develop letter recognition.

MATERIALS AND DIRECTIONS

Provide the children with some animal books to look at and find names.

Recording sheet
Crayons
Pencils

EXTENDED ACTIVITIES

* Make a class graph with the animals' names in alphabetical order.
* Older children also enjoy making an animal whose last name begins like theirs.

Animal Names

Name

LEARNING EXPERIENCE: Nocturnal Animal Book

TASK CARD

Nocturnal Animal Book

Nocturnal animals hunt at night. They use their senses.

PURPOSE: To familiarize the child with the word 'nocturnal'. An understanding of animal adaptation using senses.

MATERIALS AND DIRECTIONS

Teacher provides a booklet for each child with as many pages as appropriate. We put nocturnal chart on tagboard and laminate. The chart is available for the child's reference.

Crayons
Pencils

EXTENDED ACTIVITY

* Bat Echoes, page 30.

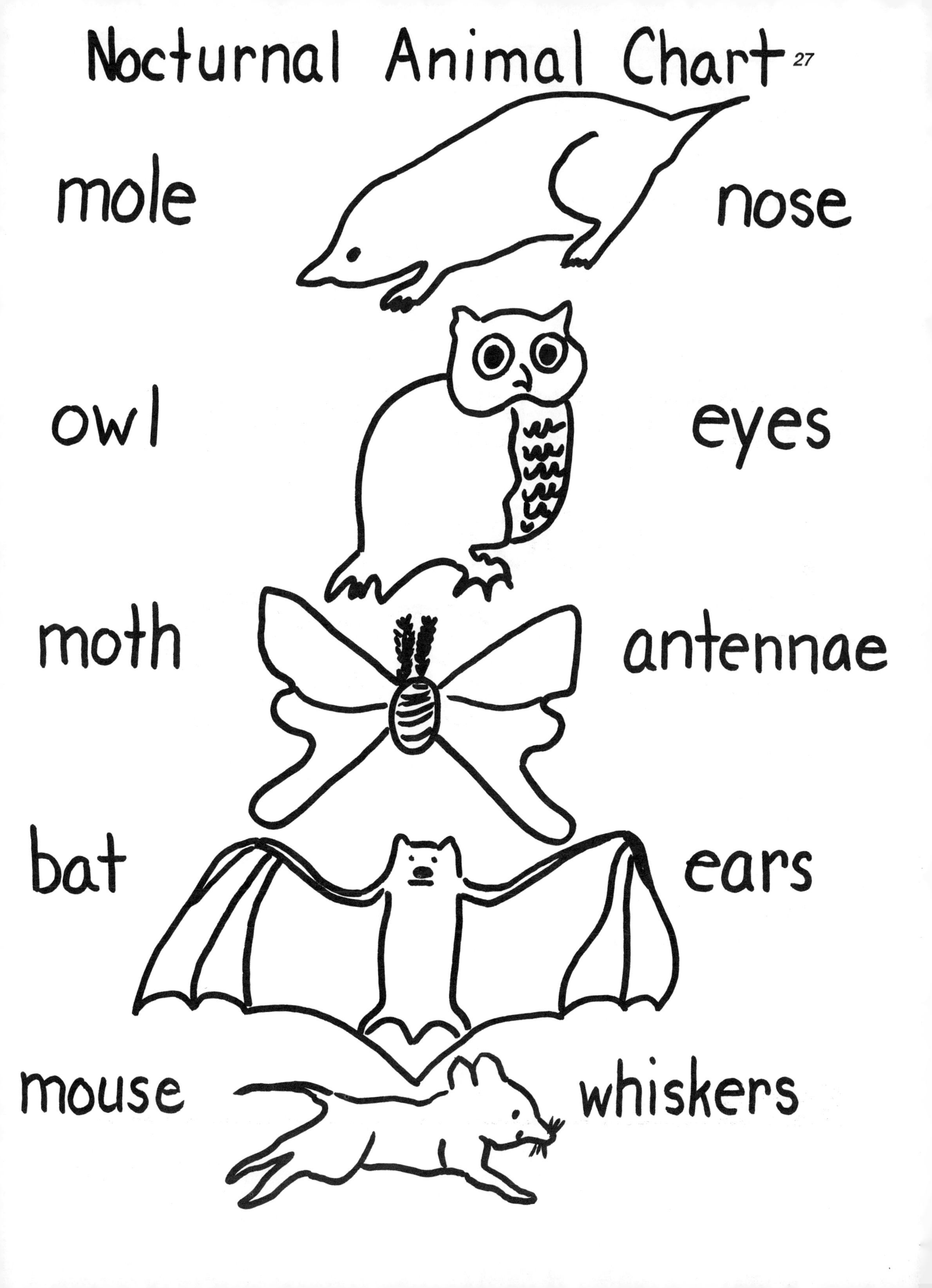
Nocturnal Animal Chart
27
mole
nose
owl
eyes
moth
antennae
bat
ears
mouse
whiskers

Nocturnal Animal Book

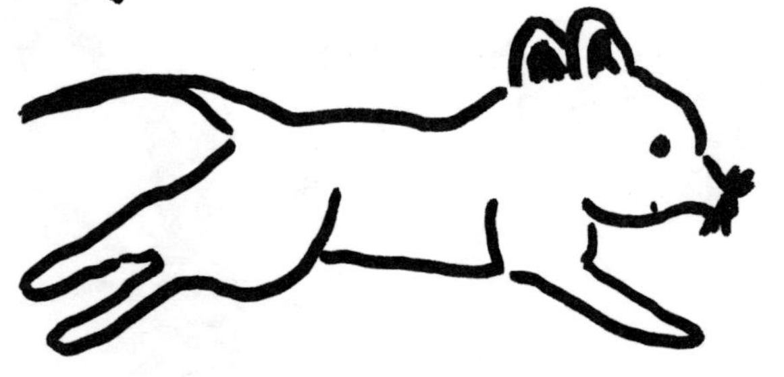

Name ______________________________

The_______uses its _______.

LEARNING EXPERIENCE: Bat Echoes

TASK CARD

Bat Echoes

The bats send out sounds as they fly. The sound hits something and bounces back to the bats. This is an ECHO.

Echo

The sound hit a moth.

PURPOSE: To develop an understanding of echoes.

MATERIALS AND DIRECTIONS

Before introducing this activity we played 'echo games' with the class. We sang the song 'Little Sir Echo' and read about echoes in books. We also talked about radar and how it works. Sonar–and how it works–is also applicable.

Recording sheet
Pencils

Crayons or pens make the sound and the echo. We had the children use blue to make the sound line from the bat and red to make the echo line.

EXTENDED ACTIVITY

* Nocturnal Animal Book, page 26.

Bat Echoes

The sound hit a ______________________.

LEARNING EXPERIENCE: Animal Tails

TASK CARD

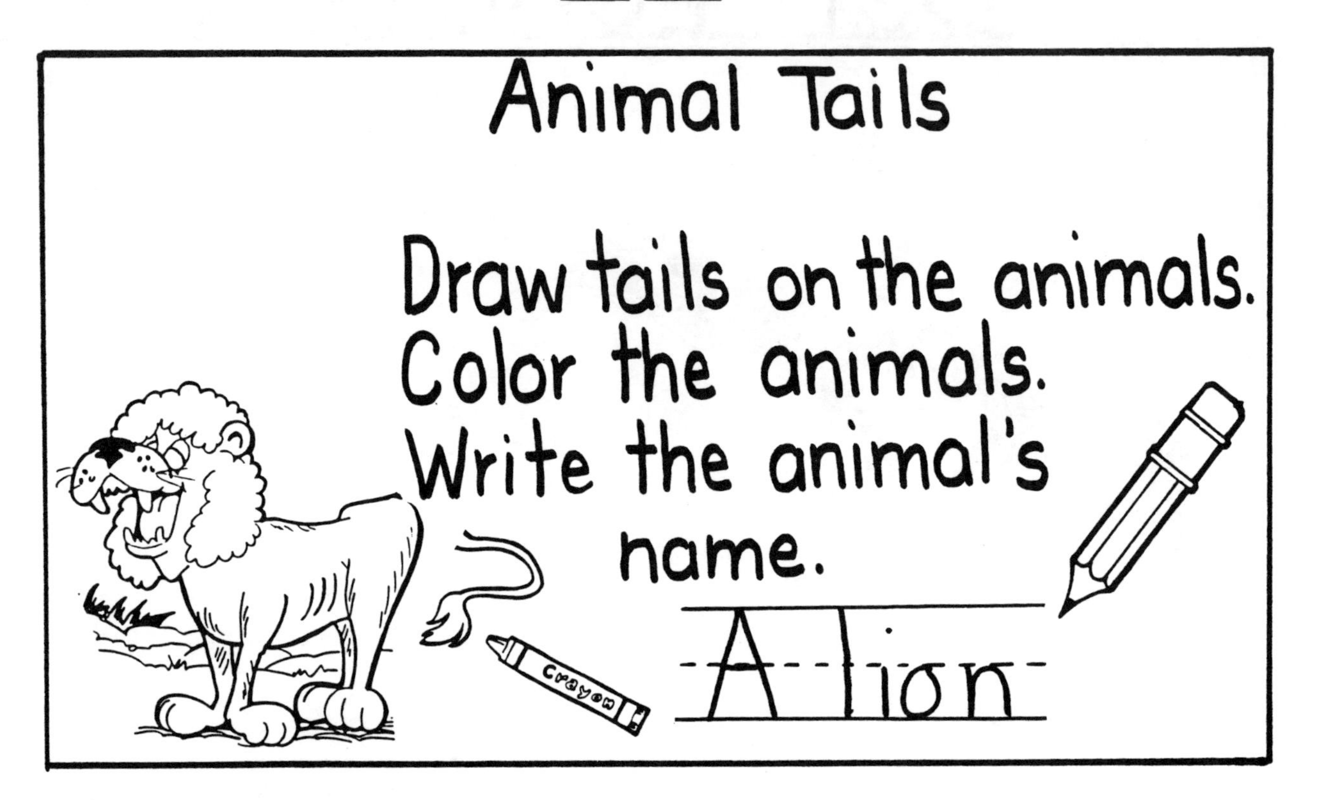

PURPOSE: Completing an animal and writing its name.

MATERIALS AND DIRECTIONS

Animal Tails Book
Pencils
Crayons

Teacher makes the Animal Tails chart for children to copy the names.

EXTENDED ACTIVITIES

* Play the game 'Pin the Tail' at circle time. We made different kinds of animal tails from paper and painted them. A child would have a tail pinned on and the other children would guess the animal's name.

* Play a variation of the above game. Children take turns describing an animal's tail. The other children guess which animal belongs to the tail just described. For instance, "I'm thinking of an animal with a bushy red tail."

Animal Tails

Draw the tails
on the animals.
Color the animals.
Write the animal's name.

My name is ______________________________

Animal Tails

tiger

horse

monkey

raccoon

sheep

LEARNING EXPERIENCE: Clay Animals

TASK CARD

PURPOSE: To provide a sensory and writing experience.

MATERIALS AND DIRECTIONS

Colored modeling clay
Paper
Pencils

EXTENDED ACTIVITY

* Children can draw pictures of the animal's habitat. These can be hung on the bulletin board along with the animal. The modeling clay, if not too thick, can be pinned with a T-pin alongside the picture or right on the picture.

LEARNING EXPERIENCE: Measure the Animals

TASK CARD

PURPOSE: To provide a measuring experience.

MATERIALS AND DIRECTIONS

Large plastic or wooden animals
Pencils
Cm cubes or another measuring tool
Recording sheet

The children are free to measure any part, or parts, of the animals. The large animals can be bought at toy stores, drug stores, or ordered from school supply catalogs.

Name ______________________________

Measure the Animals

The giraffe is ________	The elephant is ________

The zebra is ______________________

LEARNING EXPERIENCE: Which Animals Balance?

TASK CARD

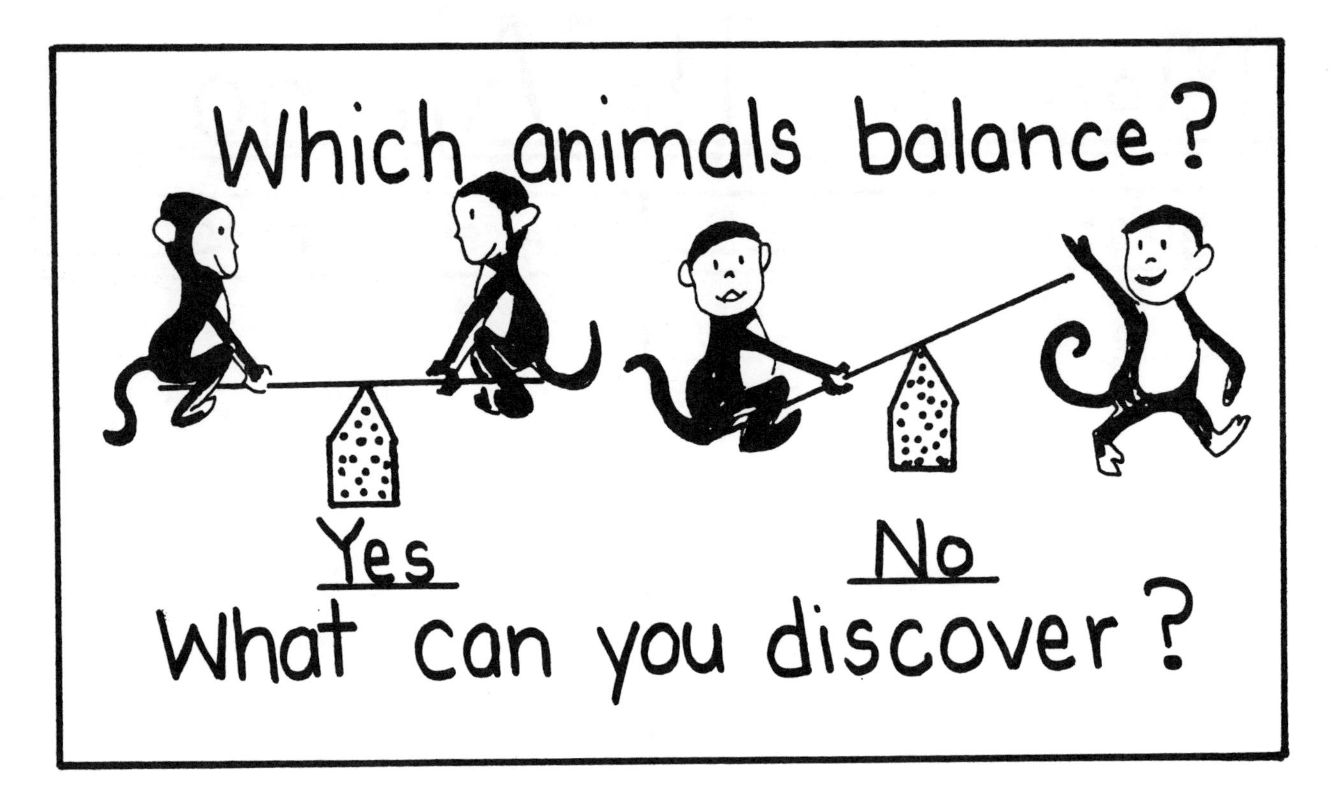

PURPOSE: To provide a balancing experience.

MATERIALS AND DIRECTIONS

Small toy animals
Balance pans
Pencils
Recording sheet

Teacher provides the children with a basket of small toy animals. The children, through trial and error, discover which animals balance. Be sure to test this activity yourself before introducing it to children. The children record what they discover as they experiment with the balance pan. They record their discoveries. Some children will want to use more than one recording sheet, so run off extras.

EXTENDED ACTIVITY

* After the children complete this activity they can experiment balancing the animals with paper clips, tooth picks, unifix cubes, . . .

Which animals balance?

Name ______________________

LEARNING EXPERIENCE: Count the Animals

TASK CARD

PURPOSE: Sorting, making equations.

MATERIALS AND DIRECTIONS

Teacher provides several small baskets of animals. Each basket should contain an assortment of wild and domestic animals. These are small plastic animals purchased in the dime store.

Recording sheet
Pencils

Count the Animals

Take a basket of animals.
Sort them, make an equation.

Wild		Domestic		Total
____	+	____	=	____
____	+	____	=	____
____	+	____	=	____
____	+	____	=	____
____	+	____	=	____

Name ________________________

LEARNING EXPERIENCE: Where Animals Live

TASK CARD

Where Animals Live

Color each animal.
Cut them out.
Put them in their homes.

PURPOSE: Matching.

MATERIALS AND DIRECTIONS

Crayons
Scissors
Glue

LEARNING EXPERIENCE: Pack Your Suitcase

TASK CARD

PURPOSE: To develop writing and thinking skills.

MATERIALS AND DIRECTIONS

Teacher runs suitcase and labels on colored construction paper. Cut small pieces of white paper 3" x 4" for children to draw items on to put in suitcase. Child cuts out and folds suitcases. Staple sides. Punch hole in tag; tie to handles of suitcase with small piece of string.

Crayons
Scissors
Pencils

Draw pictures.
Label pictures.
Put in suitcase.
Make a tag.

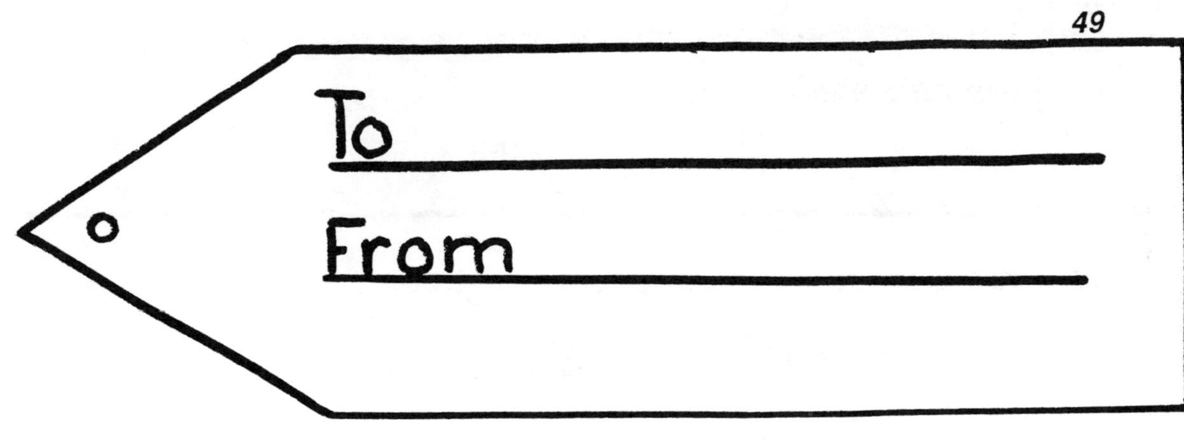
To
From

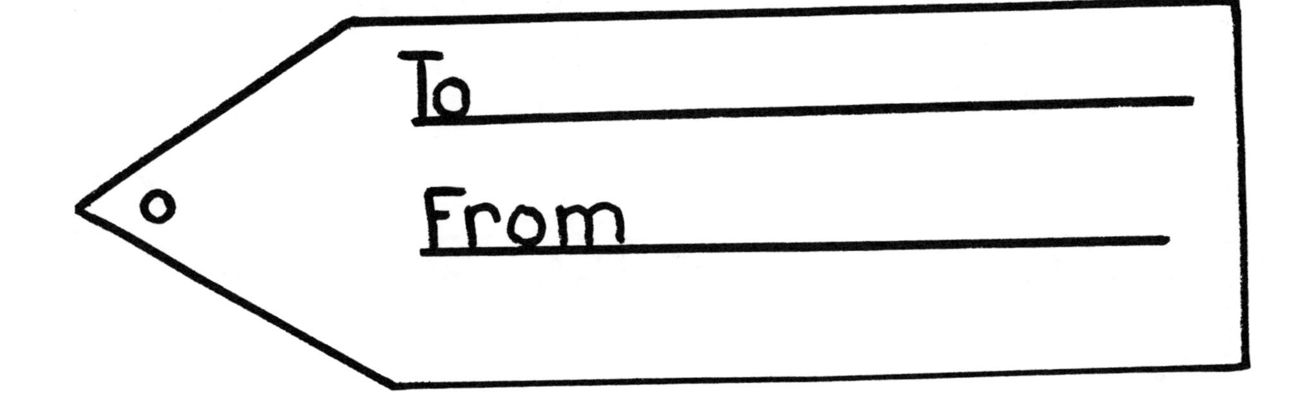
To
From

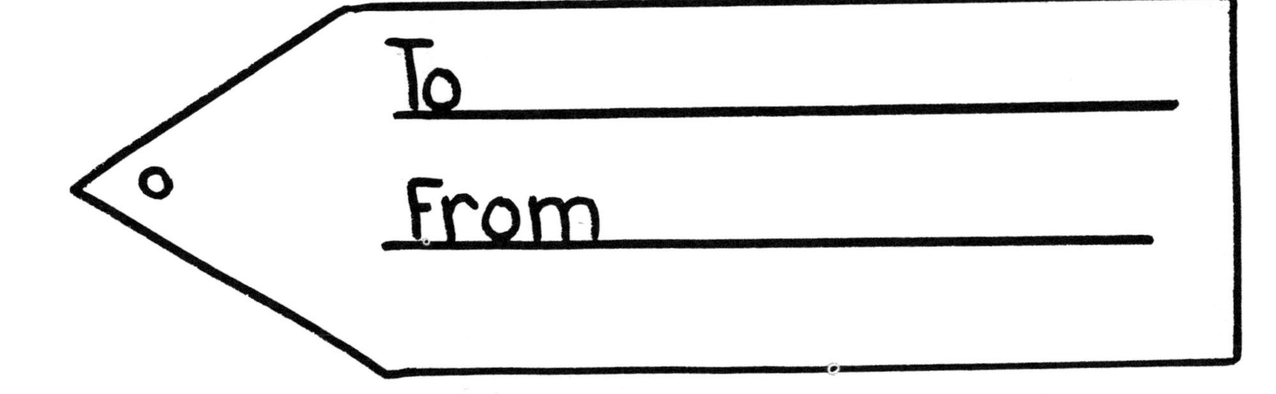
To
From

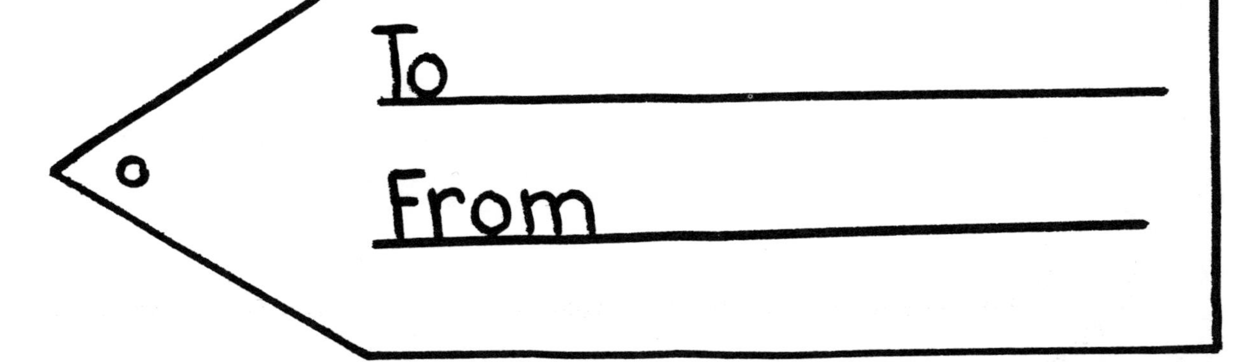
To
From

LEARNING EXPERIENCE: Who Am I?

TASK CARD

Who Am I ?

You need these words:

Squirrel Raccoon Deer

PURPOSE: To provide an opportunity in reading, writing, and matching.

MATERIALS AND DIRECTIONS

Teacher prepares booklets. Child draws animal and writes animal name.

Crayons
Pencils

EXTENDED ACTIVITY

* A "Who Am I?" game can be played at circle time. A child thinks of an animal, describes it, and then asks the class, "Who Am I?". The other children guess. This is a good game to stimulate thinking skills and provide experience in expressive language.

Who Am I ?

Name ____________________

____

This animal has antlers.
Who am I ?

This animal lives in a hollow tree.
Who am I?

This animal stores food.
Who am I?

LEARNING EXPERIENCE: Farm Full of Animals

TASK CARD

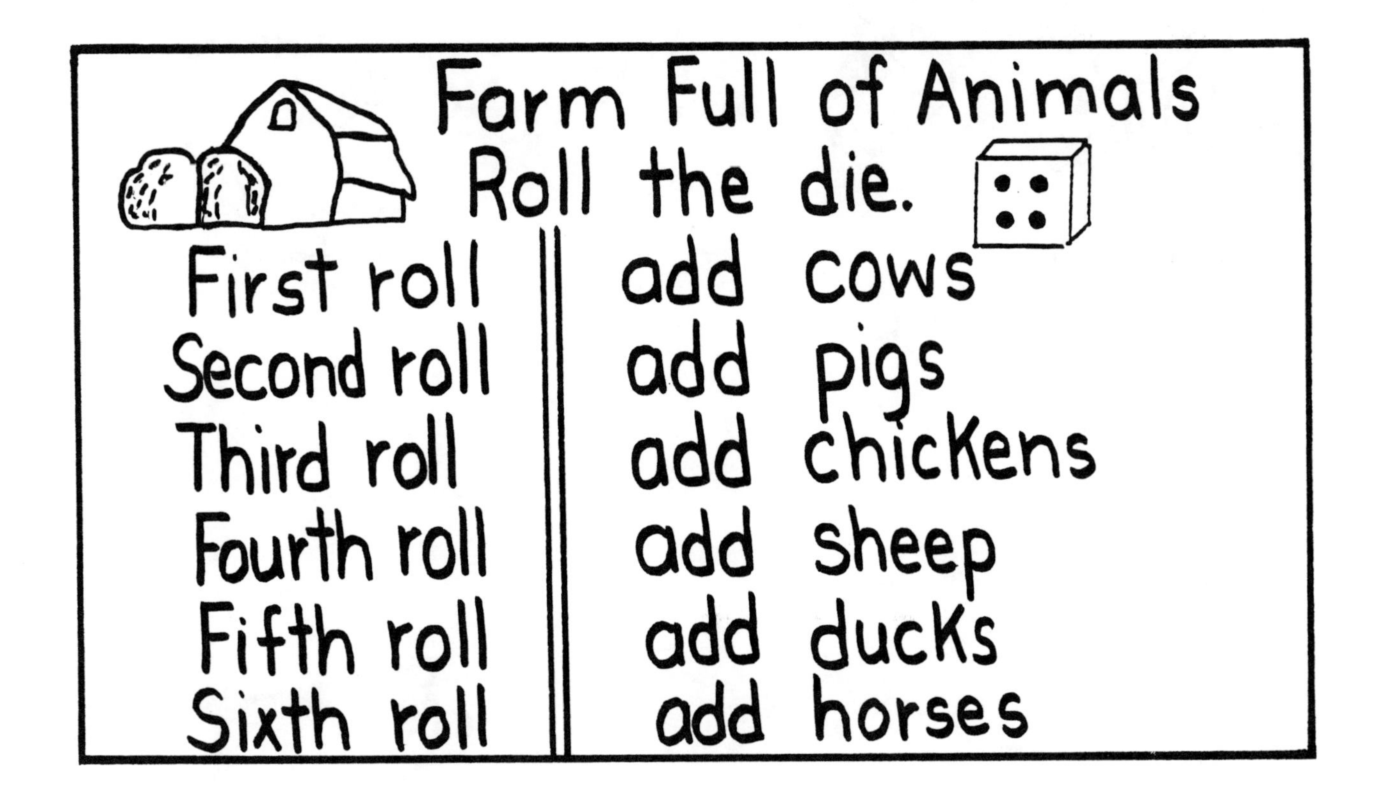

PURPOSE: To provide practice in number recognition and adding.

MATERIALS AND DIRECTIONS

Glue
Dice
Pencils
Recording sheet
Pictures of animals
12" x 18" construction paper

The child rolls the die and proceeds by following the instructions on the task card. For instance, if the first roll shows three, the child glues three cows on construction paper. If the second roll shows five, the child glues five pigs on construction paper. By the time the horses have been added to the construction paper, the farm will be full of animals!!!

Farm Full of Animals

Roll the die

First roll: ________ cows

Second roll: ________ pigs

Third roll: ________ chickens

Fourth roll: ________ sheep

Fifth roll: ________ ducks

Sixth roll: ________ horses

How many animals altogether?

____

Name ________________________

LEARNING EXPERIENCE: Elephant Treat

TASK CARD

PURPOSE: Counting and using thinking skills to create a picture.

MATERIALS AND DIRECTIONS

Peanuts — enough for each child to use five
Recording sheet
Crayons
Pencils
Glue

EXTENDED ACTIVITY

* If children are writing, have them write a story about their pictures. Younger children could write a sentence.

Elephant Treat

Take 5 peanuts.
Eat them.
Make a picture
with the shells.

LEARNING EXPERIENCE: Safari Snacks

PURPOSE: An individualized cooking experience using metric measurement.

MATERIALS AND DIRECTIONS

Teacher provides ingredients in recipe or substitutes anything that is appropriate.

Metric measuring spoons
Paper cups

This makes about a third of a cup.

Safari Snacks

25 ml granola
15 ml peanuts
5 ml raisins
2 ml sunflower seeds
2 ml coconut

Mix together.

Go on a lion hunt!

Roar-r-r

PETS

LEARNING EXPERIENCE: Pet Research

TASK CARD

PURPOSE: Clarification of the word 'research'.

MATERIALS AND DIRECTIONS

Teacher provides a variety of books about pets which are appropriate for the reading levels of children.

Paper
Paints
Pencils
Writing paper
Scissors

After the child paints the picture of his/her pet, it is cut out and pinned on the bulletin board. For the child who can read, a book is read about that pet and then the child proceeds to write a report about the pet. For the child who is not reading, a report can still be written based on the child's knowledge of his/her pet.

We have a discussion about pets before this activity is introduced. Some children will not have a pet. We say to the children, "Some people do not have pets. What would you choose if you did have one?" Or, we suggest that they choose one of our classroom pets to draw and write about.

On page 63, there are two notes which we sent home with the children — one for readers and one for non-readers. The lines were filled in with the child's name and the pet he/she wrote about. Several parents came by to look at the children's work. A very positive experience!

EXTENDED ACTIVITIES

* Make a class graph of pets. Each child said what kind of a pet or pets he/she has. A column on the graph was then marked with that pet's name — cat, dog, turtle. A square was colored in opposite the name each time that pet was mentioned. We then 'read the graph' by finding out how many people have dogs, cats, etc.; which pet do we have the most of, the least of; which ones are reptiles, mammals. This discussion resulted in many questions and comments from the children.

* Use the 'Spelling Cup' idea which can be found in our SPACE and SEA LIFE books. Place pet names in the cups and have children spell them and draw pictures.

Sample of note sent home with non-readers.

<u>Ann</u> made a picture of <u>her</u> pet. <u>She</u> also wrote a report. Both are displayed on our class bulletin board. We invite you to come and see. Date________

Sample sent home with readers.

<u>Ann</u> made a picture of <u>her</u> pet. <u>She</u> also read a book about <u>cats</u> and wrote a report. Both are displayed on our class bulletin board. We invite you to come and see. Date________

LEARNING EXPERIENCE: Draw a Pet

TASK CARD

PURPOSE: To provide practice in forming equations.

MATERIALS AND DIRECTIONS

Dice
Recording sheet
Pencils
Crayons

Children record ONLY the equations that respond to the sum on the task card. As they record their equations they draw what the directions on the task card tells them to draw.

This activity can be designed for the young child by using only one die. Change the task card to correspond to numbers 1 through 6. The purpose of the learning experience then becomes practice in number recognition.

Name ______________________

Draw a Pet

Make the body shape.
Roll the dice and add.

Write the equations

______________ ______________

______________ ______________

______________ ______________

______________ ______________

Draw pet here

LEARNING EXPERIENCE: Pet Store

TASK CARD

PURPOSE: Decision making and adding.

MATERIALS AND DIRECTIONS

Pictures of 'Pets to Choose" – precut for young child
Recording sheet
Pencils
Cubes, toothpicks or some other objects to assist children in adding
Glue

Children are free to choose as many pets as they want. If this is a problem, limit the number. Some children may use more than one recording sheet to glue their pets on.

EXTENDED ACTIVITIES

* Have children write the names of the pets they chose on another piece of paper – for instance, dog, bird, turtle. Or if they choose more than one of something, have them record the number – for instance, 2 dogs, 5 birds, 3 turtles.

* Have children choose pets which add up to 50 or 100! No more, no less.

Pets to choose

Pet Store

These are the pets in my store.
My name is ______________________

What are all the pets in your store worth?

____
answer

LEARNING EXPERIENCE: Choose a Pet

TASK CARD

Choose a Pet

Draw any supplies you will need.

PURPOSE: Decision making.

MATERIALS AND DIRECTIONS

Teacher prepares pet pictures so child can choose one. Child glues picture on recording sheet and draws the supplies needed by the pet.

Recording sheet
Pet pictures
Crayons
Glue

Name ______________________________

Pet Store

I chose a ______________________

LEARNING EXPERIENCE: Cricket Observation

TASK CARD

Cricket Observation
Work with a partner.
Observe the cricket and record.

PURPOSE: To provide an opportunity for observation skills and recording.

NOTE: We have found field crickets to be an acceptable classroom pet. They can be purchased at pet stores. We paid 6 cents per cricket.

MATERIALS AND DIRECTIONS

Field crickets
Magnifying glasses
Cricket recording book
Pencils
Crayons
Container and supplies for crickets

Before we introduced this activity, we bought six crickets and had them in a container for the children to observe as pets. This is what our cricket container looked like:

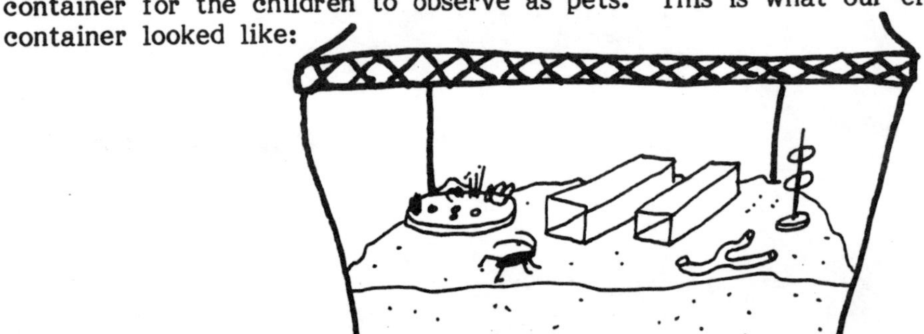

We read books about crickets and had discussions about crickets.

We had the children work with a partner in order to provide a time for cooperative interaction. We placed one cricket in a large jar with a top which had holes in it. Each set of partners got a cricket to observe. We put a piece of sliced cucumber in the jar with the cricket so there would be food and moisture available. Upon completion of this learning experience we released the crickets in a nearby field.

EXTENDED ACTIVITIES

* Measure the Cricket, page 76.
* Buying Crickets, page 79.

Cricket Observation

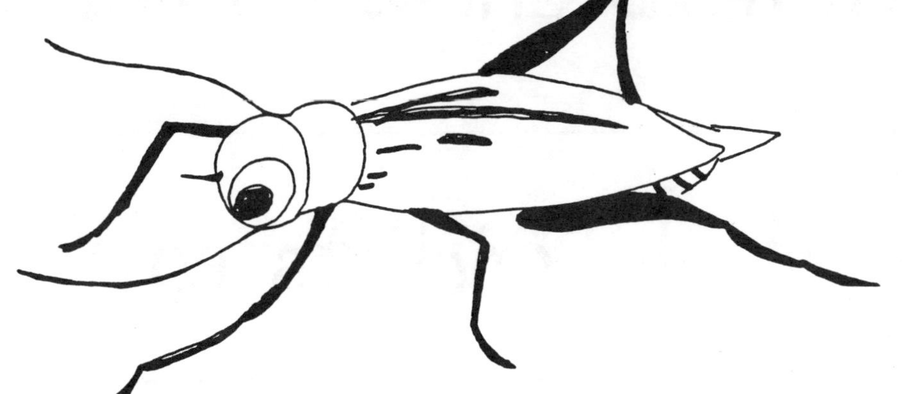

My name: ______________________

My partner's name: ______________________

Look at the abdomen.

Is your cricket male or female?

____

Draw a male cricket	Draw a female cricket

Habitat

Where do crickets live?

____

What do crickets eat?

____

____

____

Do crickets live in your neighborhood?

____

Listen to the cricket.

What Kind of sound does it make?

____

How does it make the sound?

____

____

Look at the whole cricket.

Is it the same color all over?

____

Write the color names.

____

____

____

____

Draw the whole cricket.

Give your cricket a name:

____

LEARNING EXPERIENCE: Measure the Cricket

TASK CARD

Measure the Cricket

Record your findings.

The thorax is 5 cm.

PURPOSE: To provide a measuring experience.

MATERIALS AND DIRECTIONS

Picture of cricket to measure
Cm cubes
Recording sheet
Pencils

Teacher glues picture of cricket to measure on tag and laminates. We prepare 4 crickets for this activity.

EXTENDED ACTIVITIES:

* Cricket Observation, page 72.
* Buying Crickets, page 79.

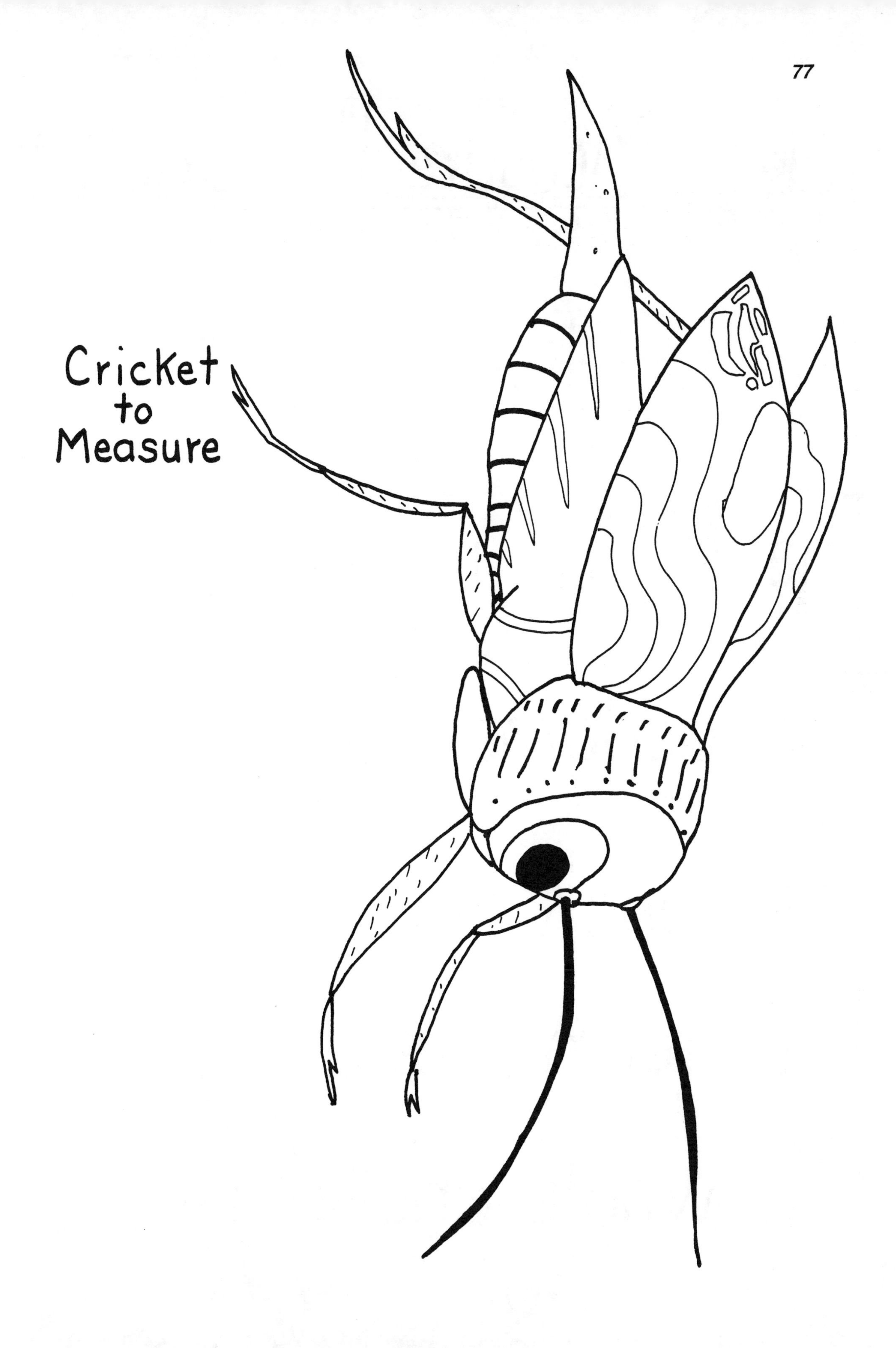
Cricket
to
Measure

Measure the Cricket

The head is ______________

The thorax is ______________

The abdomen is ______________

The back leg is ______________

1 antenna is ______________

The whole cricket is ______________

LEARNING EXPERIENCE: Buying Crickets

TASK CARD

Buying Crickets

Six crickets cost 36¢

How many ways can you make 36¢?

Use the money.

6¢

10¢

1¢

5¢

25¢

PURPOSE: To reinforce concept of coin values and combinations.

NOTE: Since our class had bought six crickets at 6¢ each, this activity was designed around the sum 36 cents.

MATERIALS AND DIRECTIONS

Recording book
Pencils
Paper money
Glue

We precut the coins and had them in four containers: nickels, dimes, pennies, and quarters. The children proceeded to select any combination of 36 cents they could think of, take those coins and glue them on the page. The book will contain as many pages as combinations the child can think of.

EXTENDED ACTIVITIES

* Cricket Observation, page 72.
* Measure the Cricket, page 76.

Buying Crickets

Buy 6 crickets.

What money will you use?

Name ______________________________

______________________________ = 36¢

Money for buying crickets

LEARNING EXPERIENCE: Bunny Rabbit Carrots

PURPOSE: To provide the child with an individualized cooking experience.

MATERIALS AND DIRECTIONS

Teacher brings carrots with tops on for the children.

Container to wash carrots
Potato peelers

Bunny Rabbit Carrots

Wash a carrot.
Scrape a carrot.
Eat a carrot.

ENDANGERED AND EXTINCT ANIMALS

Following are the definitions of certain words used in these learning experiences:

Environment—the total of all the surroundings that have influence on someone or something.
Endangered—in danger of extinction.
Extinct—no longer existing; removed from existence.
Habitat—the place where an animal is normally or naturally found, including food, water, shelter, space.

Additional information on endangered and extinct animals can be obtained from various sources: books, magazines, films, and public and private agencies. Project WILD (Wildlife in Learning Design), for instance, is an education program of instructional workshops and supplementary curriculum materials. Project WILD stresses the interrelationship between people and wildlife and the responsibility of people to share the earth. Project WILD is sponsored nationally by the Western Association of Fish and Wildlife Agencies, Salina Star Route, Boulder, Colorado 80302 (telephone 303-444-2390).

The filmstrip series *Our Vanishing Wildlife* is excellent. In particular, the one entitled "Our Wild Friends: It's Not Too Late to Care" is appropriate for primary and elementary grades. Write to Pomfret House, Pomfret Center, Connecticut 06259.

LEARNING EXPERIENCE: Endangered or Extinct

TASK CARD

Endangered or Extinct?

Cut out the letters.
Put the word together.

Define the word.
List some animals.

panda

PURPOSE: To clarify and define the words, ENDANGERED and EXTINCT.

MATERIALS AND DIRECTIONS

Scissors
Pencils
Glue
Letter page
2 Recording pages

Children cut out the letters for the words 'endangered' and 'extinct'. These letters are glued in the boxes on the recording page. The definition is then written and four animals listed in each category.

Courtesy of Teri Cocita, co-teacher with Ann Packard

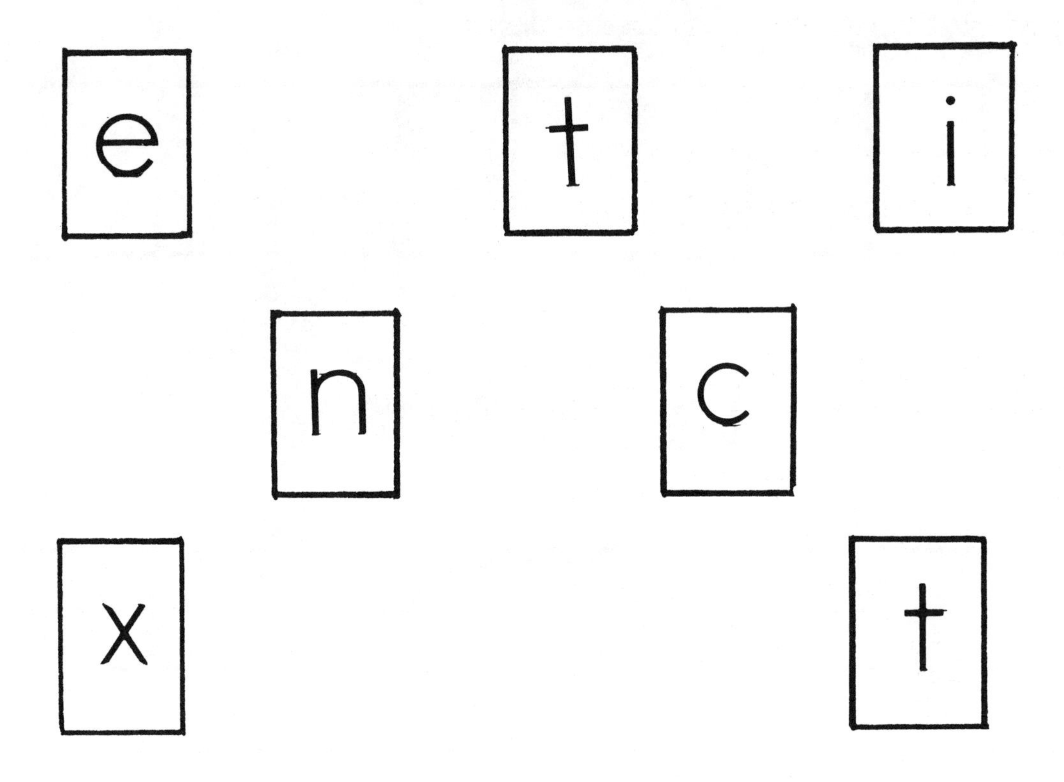
e
t
i
n
c
x
t

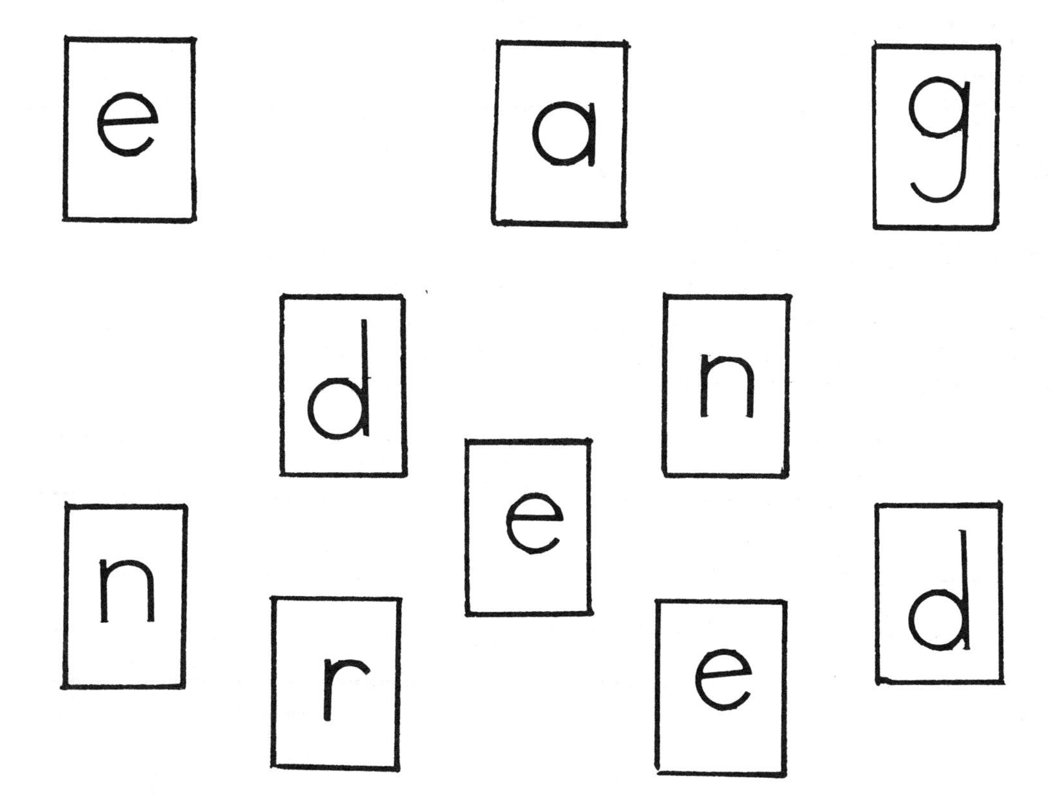
e
a
g
d
n
e
n
r
e
d

Word

Definition

List of Animals

Word

Definition

List of Animals

LEARNING EXPERIENCE: Bring Back 3 Extinct Animals

TASK CARD

Bring back three extinct animals.
Put the puzzle together.

What is the animal's name?
How did it become extinct?

PURPOSE: To identify extinct animals.

MATERIALS AND DIRECTIONS

Run puzzle pictures on 3 different colors of construction paper. Cut into appropriate number of pieces for the children. We cut them into 5 pieces for the young child and paper clip the pieces together.

9" x 12" construction paper to glue puzzle pieces onto
Staple recording sheet on back
Glue
Scissors
Crayons
Pencils

INFORMATION SHEET ON THESE THREE EXTINCT ANIMALS

The Dodo was a flightless bird living on the island of Mauritius. Humans brought pigs, rats and monkeys to the island. These animals and the sailors hunted and ate the birds and their eggs. The last Dodo was seen in the 1600's.

Passenger Pigeons lived in the forests of the Midwest. Early settlers cut down the trees. The birds became pests to the farmers; many were shot or poisoned. The last one died in a zoo in 1914.

The Great Auk lived on Artic islands; it was a fine swimmer, but was flightless. The skins were highly prized in Europe. They were hunted to extinction by 1844.

Bring back 3 extinct animals.

Put the puzzle together.

What is the animal's name?

How did it become extinct?

PASSENGER PIGEON

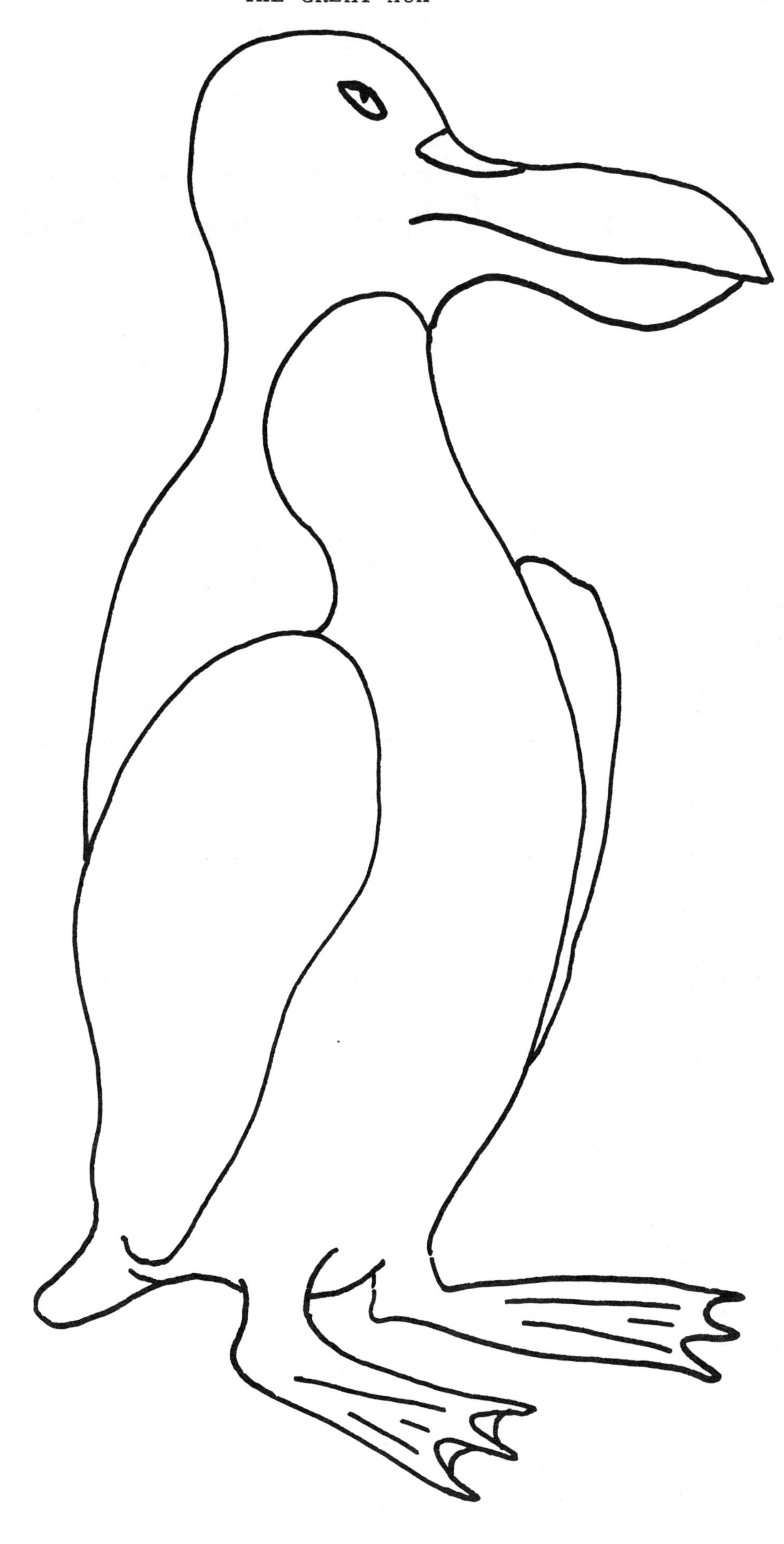

LEARNING EXPERIENCE: Book of Endangered Animals

TASK CARD

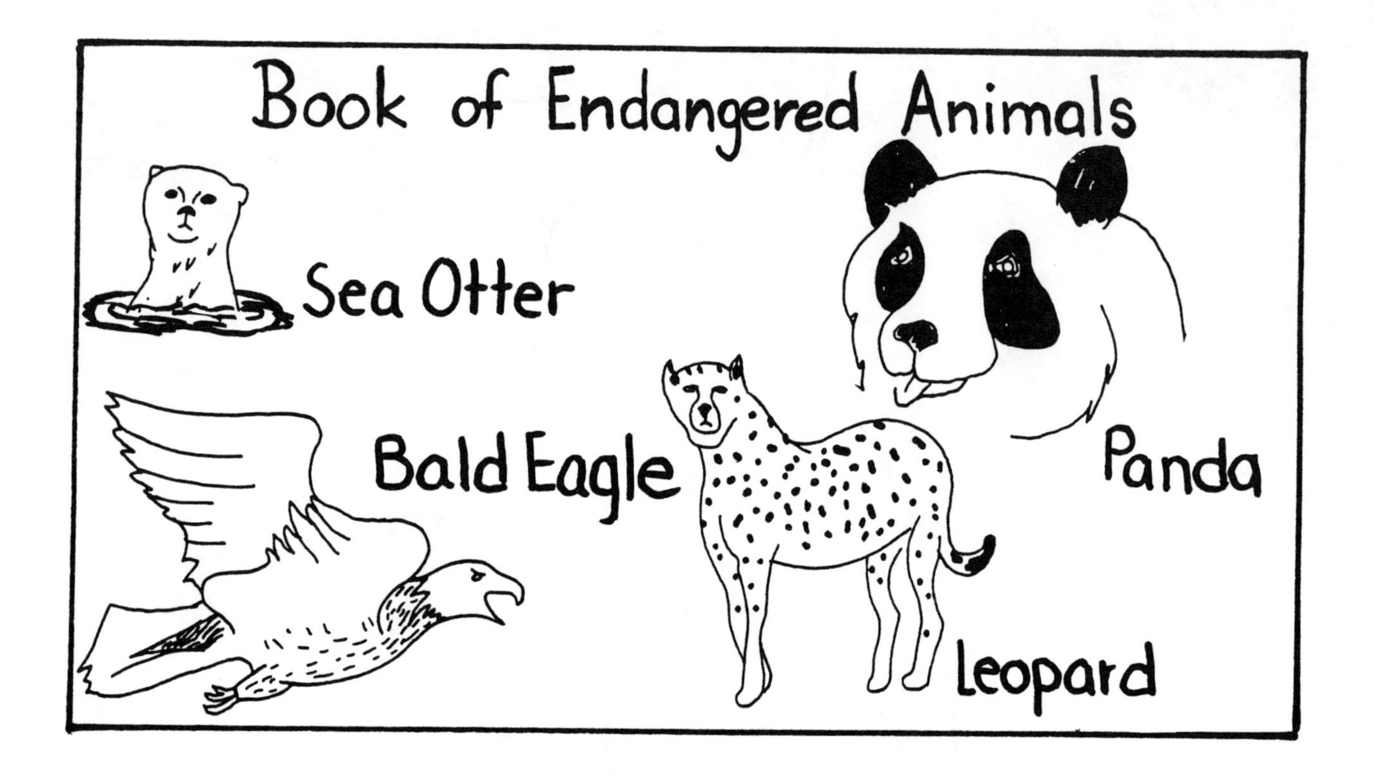

PURPOSE: To provide information about endangered animals.

MATERIALS AND DIRECTIONS

Teacher prepares Endangered Animal Book for each child. Child refers to information on task card, draws animals and writes animal names.

Crayons
Pencils

Book of Endangered Animals

by ______________________________

I am very fast.

My spots help me hide.

I am endangered.

I am a bird of prey.

I am America's symbol.

I am an endangered animal.

I eat crabs and abalone.

I like to float in kelp beds.

I am an endangered animal.

I am black and white.

I eat bamboo. I live in China.

I am an endangered animal.

LEARNING EXPERIENCE: Animal Needs

TASK CARD

Animal Needs

Animals need food, water, shelter and space, or they will become endangered.

Think of a wild animal.
Create a healthy environment.

PURPOSE: To reinforce an awareness of animal needs.

MATERIALS AND DIRECTIONS

9" x 12" manila paper for drawing the picture
Crayons
Pencils
Recording sheet
Assortment of animal books for the child to gather information

Upon completion of this learning experience we stapled the children's recording sheets to their pictures and displayed them on the bulletin board.

Animal Needs

Complete the sentences after you have made your picture.

1. My animal is a ________________.
2. My animal gets water from ________________________________.
3. My animal eats ________________.
4. My animal is sheltered by ________________________________.
5. My animal's space is ________________________________.

My name is ________________.

LEARNING EXPERIENCE: Value of My Arrangement

TASK CARD

PURPOSE: To reinforce the value of animal needs using addition and subtraction.

MATERIALS AND DIRECTIONS

Scissors
Crayons
Glue
Pencils
Arrangement pictures
9" x 12" light blue construction paper
Recording sheet

The pictures for the arrangement were run on white construction paper so the children could color them. They were then glued onto the light blue construction paper.

You can give each picture in the arrangement any value. We used a total value of 50. The water was 20, food was 15, shelter was 10, space was 5. These values were written directly on each arrangement picture.

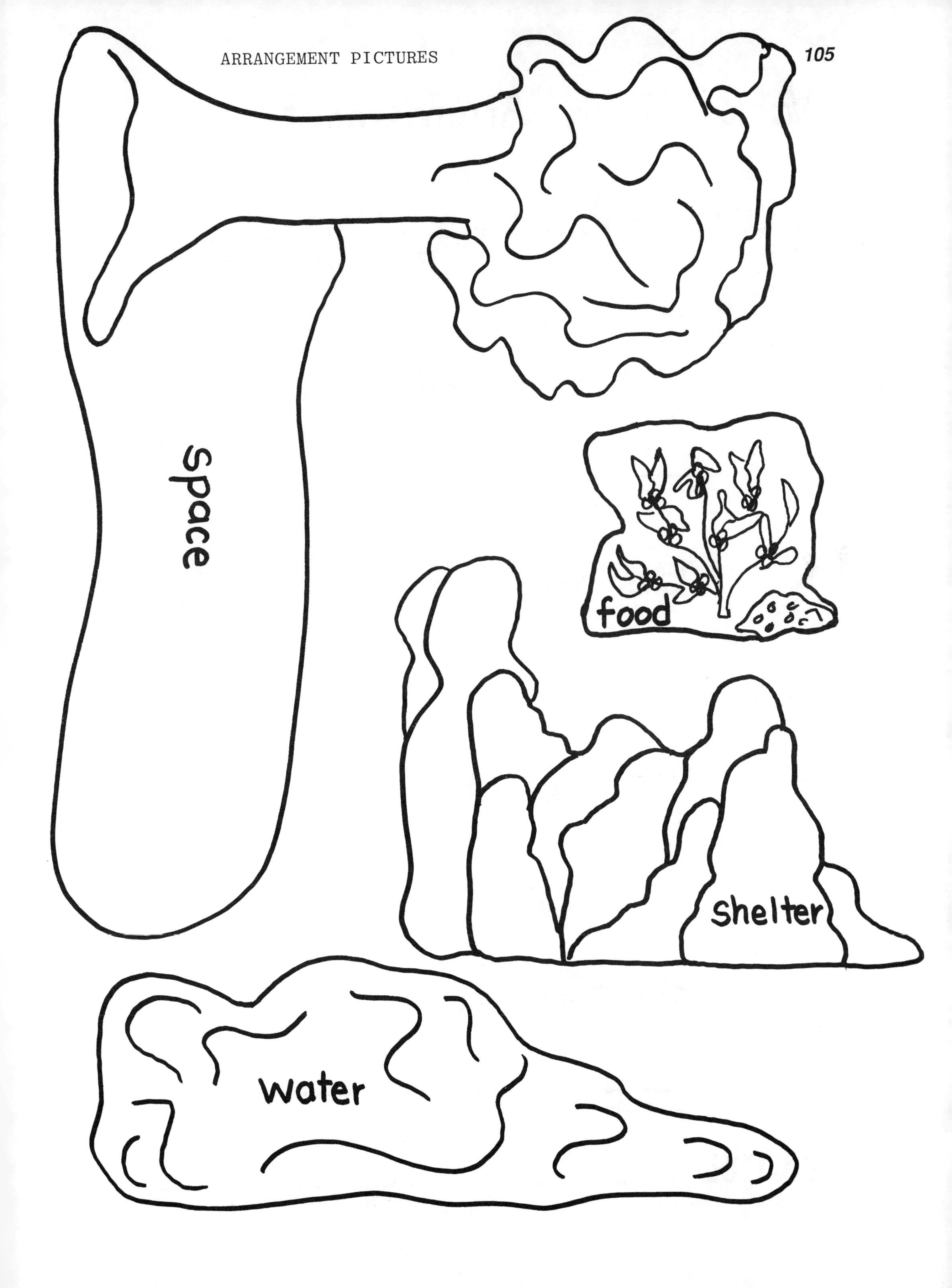
space
food
shelter
water

Value Of My Arrangement

_____ + _____ + _____ + _____ = _____
water food shelter space total value

Take away water:

_____ - _____ = _____
total value water

Take away food:

_____ - _____ = _____
total value food

Take away shelter:

_____ - _____ = _____
total value shelter

Take away space:

_____ - _____ = _____
total value space

Name ____________________

LEARNING EXPERIENCE: Endangered Animals

TASK CARD

Endangered Animals

Choose a card.
Draw the animal.
Continue to add one more endangered animal to your picture.
Record the animal names.

PURPOSE: To familiarize the children with endangered animals through drawing, writing and adding one more.

MATERIALS AND DIRECTIONS

Endangered animal cards
Pencils
9" x 12" construction paper to draw their pictures
Recording sheet for writing

Teacher prepares endangered animal cards from pictures on page 108.
Cut them out, glue them on tag, and laminate.
The children choose the cards, one at a time, and proceed to 'add one more' to their picture.
Upon completion of the picture, the children then write the names of the animals they drew on recording sheet.

Endangered Animals

Brown Bear

Ocelot

Polar Bear

Bald Eagle

Manatee

Brown Pelican

Blue Whale

Sea Otter

Panda

These are the endangered animals in my picture.

Name

LEARNING EXPERIENCE: Orangutans in Danger

TASK CARD

PURPOSE: To provide an awareness of endangered animals and provide practice in subtraction.

MATERIALS AND DIRECTIONS

Rain Forest cards
Orangutan cards
Recording sheet
Pencils
2 Containers

Teacher prepares rain forest and orangutan cards. Run off, glue on tag, laminate, and cut apart. Place cards in two separate containers. The child takes a rain forest card, records the number; takes an orangutan card, records the number. The child then subtracts to find out 'how many orangutans left'. We prepared this activity for practice in subtraction under ten. You can change the numerals on the cards to meet your children's needs.

EXTENDED ACTIVITY

* This learning experience can be designed using seals, whales, or any other animals in danger.

Courtesy of Teri Cocita, co-teacher with Ann Packard

Orangutans in Danger

The rain forests are being cut down. The orangutan is in danger.

Take the cards.
Write the equation.

orangutan		rain forest		How many left ?
______	–	______	=	______
______	–	______	=	______
______	–	______	=	______
______	–	______	=	______
______	–	______	=	______
______	–	______	=	______
______	–	______	=	______

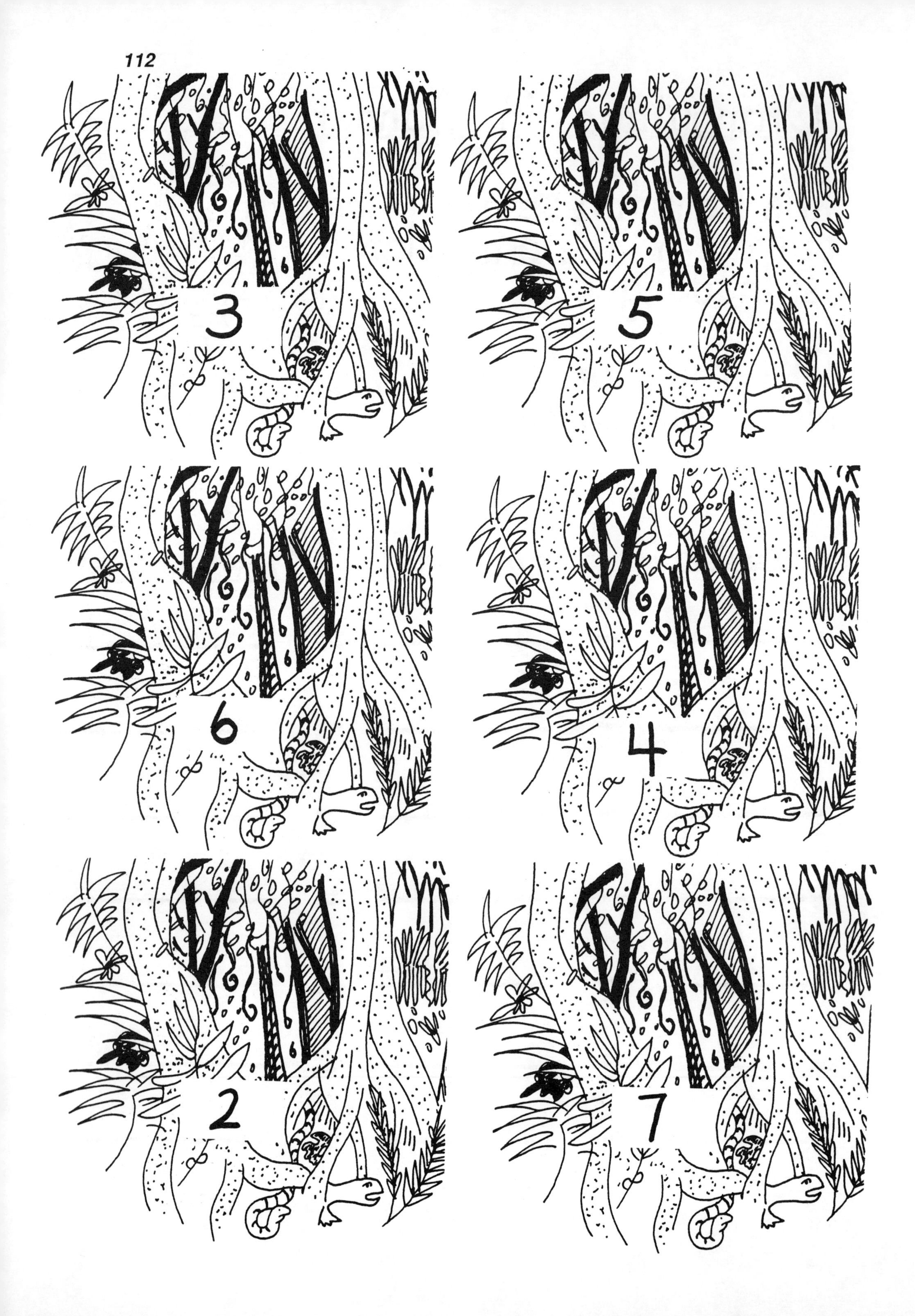
3
5
6
4
2
7

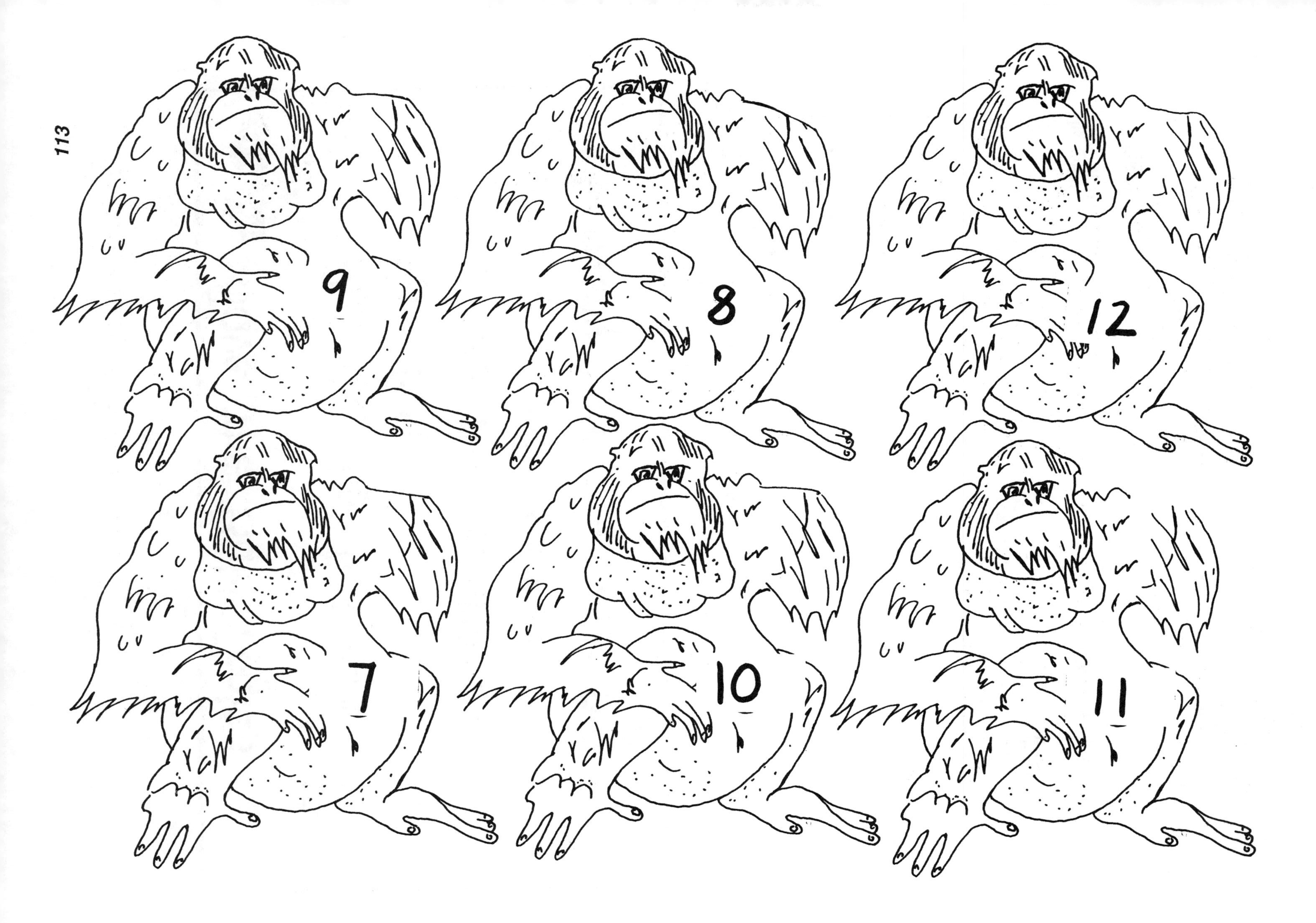
9
8
12
7
10
11

LEARNING EXPERIENCE: Save the Bald Eagles

TASK CARD

Save the Bald Eagles

Roll the die 5 times.

Add Eagles.

Record the numbers.

5 + 1 + 2 + 4 + 1 = 13

How many Eagles in your picture?

PURPOSE: To practice counting and adding.

MATERIALS AND DIRECTIONS

Dice
Recording sheet
Sitting eagles
Flying eagles
12" x 18" manila paper
Glue
Scissors

Teacher runs off sitting and flying eagles. These can be precut for the young child. As the child rolls the die, the number is recorded on recording sheet. The child then selects that number of sitting or flying eagles. For instance, if the die reads 4, the child may select 4 sitting eagles or 4 flying eagles. The eagles are then glued on the manila paper. The child continues rolling the die until five rolls have been completed. At the completion of the five rolls, the child looks at his/her paper and counts 'how many flying eagles' and 'how many sitting eagles' and records.

EXTENDED ACTIVITY

* This learning experience can be designed using other endangered animals.

Name ______________________________

These are the numbers I rolled:

___ + ___ + ___ + ___ + ___ = ___

How many eagles sitting? ________

How many eagles flying? ________

Name ______________________________

These are the numbers I rolled:

___ + ___ + ___ + ___ + ___ = ___

How many eagles sitting? ________

How many eagles flying? ________

Flying Eagles

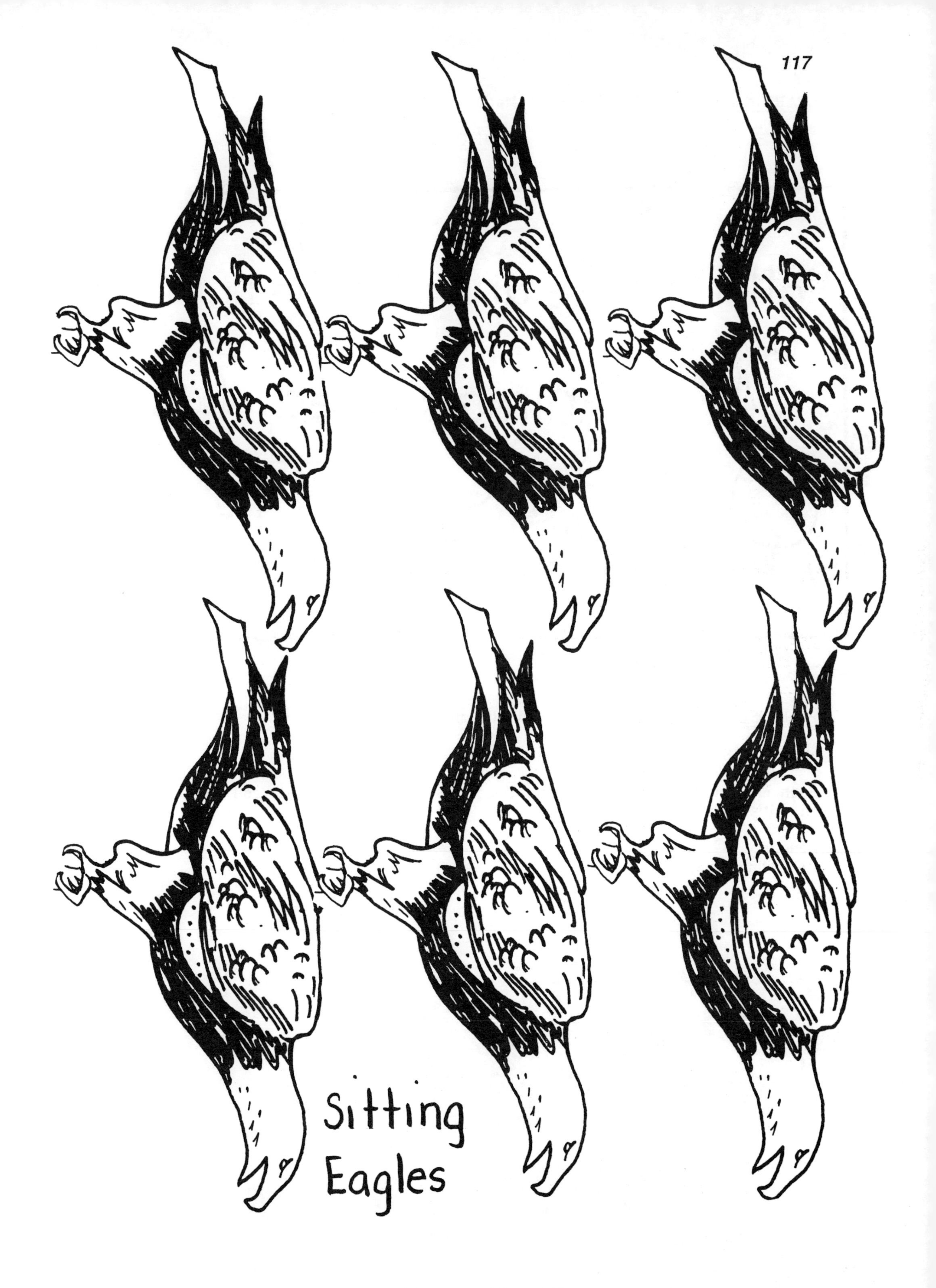
Sitting
Eagles

LEARNING EXPERIENCE: Habitat Math

TASK CARD

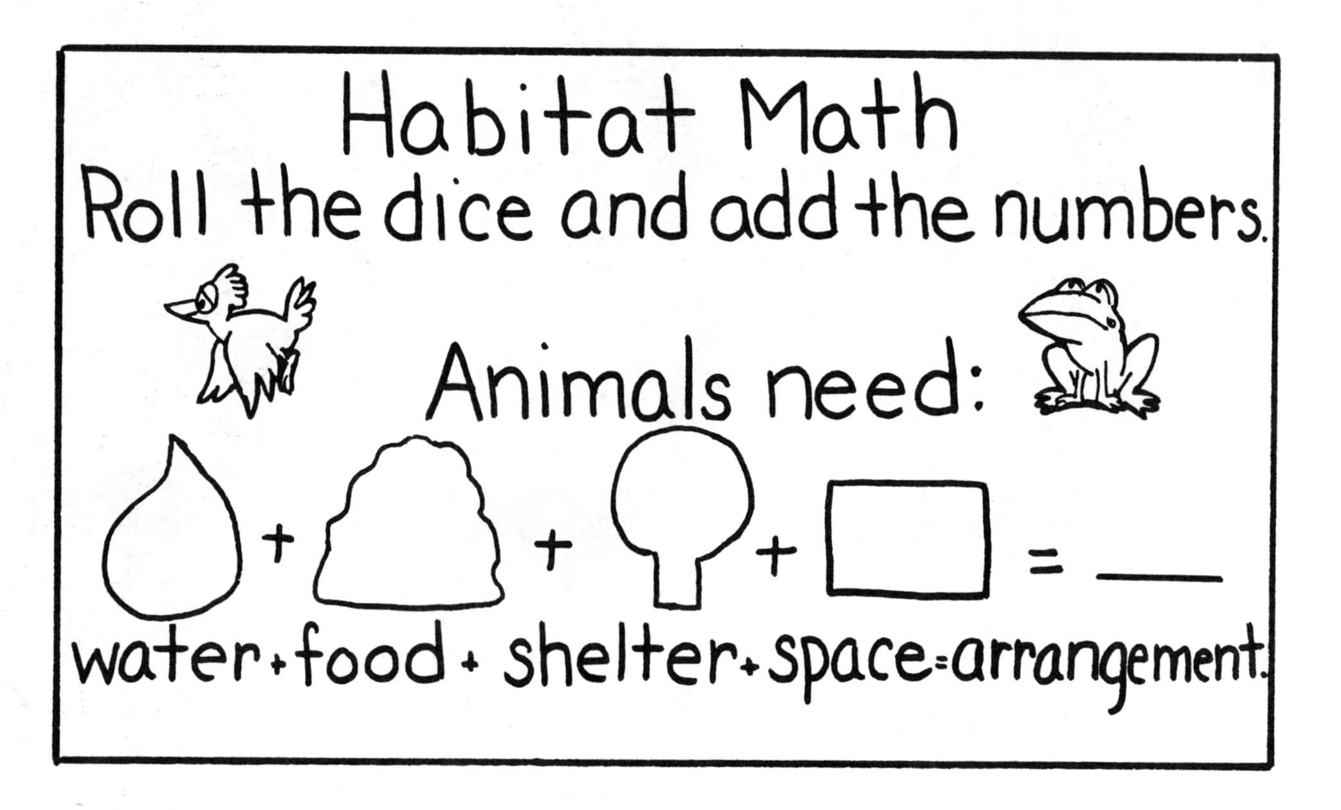

PURPOSE: To identify animal needs utilizing addition.

MATERIALS AND DIRECTIONS

Each child needs 4 dice. We use felt squares for the children to roll the dice on — it's quieter!

Pencils
Recording sheet

Habitat Math

Name: ______________________________

Animals need water, food, shelter, and space. Roll the dice and add.

+ + + = ______

+ + + = ______

+ + + = ______

+ + + = ______

+ + + = ______

+ + + = ______

water + food + shelter + space = arrangement

LEARNING EXPERIENCE: Habitat Dice Roll

TASK CARD

PURPOSE: To reinforce number recognition and an awareness of animal needs.

MATERIALS AND DIRECTIONS

Teacher prepares animal patterns. Child chooses an animal when he/she rolls 1. Continue by drawing other parts of the habitat as the die is rolled.

Recording sheet
Crayons
Scissors

Animal Patterns

Habitat Dice Roll

Name ______________________

LEARNING EXPERIENCE: Our Bird Sanctuary

TASK CARD

Our Bird Sanctuary

Choose a bird card.
Read the card.
Make a bird for our sanctuary.

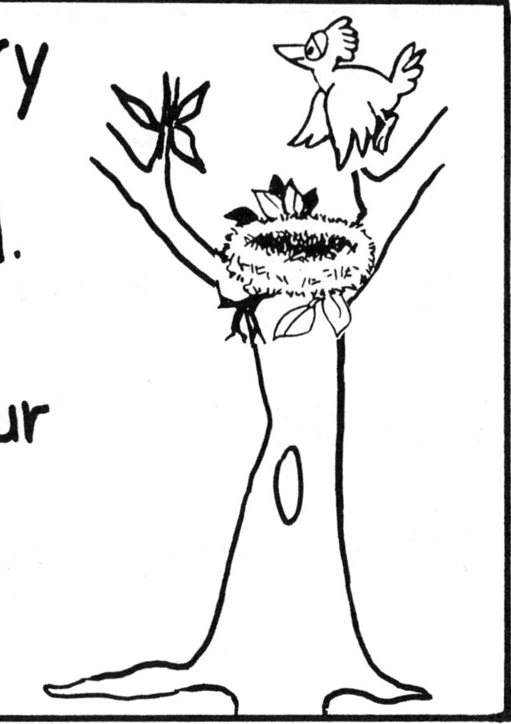

PURPOSE: To provide practice in reading.

MATERIALS AND DIRECTIONS

Bird reading cards
Easel paper
Paints
Stapler
Scissors

Children make dimensional birds to hang in the sanctuary. After painting both sides of the bird, the two sheets of paper are stapled and stuffed.

Courtesy of Teri Cocita, co-teacher with Ann Packard

California Condor

The California Condor lives in high mountains. There are only 50 left in North America because they have been hunted.

Brown Pelican

The pelican is one of the largest flying birds. It can hold 3 gallons in its pouch. Their nests and breeding grounds are being destroyed.

DucK

DucKs are good swimmers. They have webbed feet. Some ducks are in danger because of pollution in rivers and lakes.

Trumpeter Swan

The trumpeter swan is a large bird with a beautiful long neck. This swan was hunted for its soft down. It is now protected by law.

LEARNING EXPERIENCE: Dodo Bird's Egg Salad

PURPOSE: To provide the child with an individualized cooking experience.

MATERIALS AND DIRECTIONS:

Teacher prepares egg salad and furnishes other recipe ingredients.

Dodo Bird's Egg Salad

Spread egg salad on a slice of bread.

Add 1 cucumber slice to your bread.

TEDDY BEARS
AND OTHER STUFFED ANIMALS

Pages 132 and 133 are two sample invitations for Stuffed Animal Day and Bear Day. When the children bring their animals in bags, each child is encouraged to give clues about his or her animal while the classmates guess. Then the bag is opened, revealing the animal.

During circle or group time, the children each introduce their animals, giving information such as the animal's type, name, and age. As the child shares the animal, we provide a name tag for the child to attach to the animal. All the animals sit on a special blanket and visit while the children have their worktime.

As teachers we also bring a teddy bear or other stuffed animal to share, plus one or two extras for those children who may have forgotten to bring animals or just don't have any.

Bring your favorite stuffed animal to school tomorrow. Bring it in a paper bag so that we can guess what it is.

Math games

Guess who?

Anns Animal

Stories

Songs

Cooking

Invite your bear to school.
Your bear can meet your teacher.
Your bear can visit other bears.
Your bear can taste porridge
with honey. It's a Bear Party!

LEARNING EXPERIENCE: Bear Reading Cards

TASK CARD

Bear Reading Cards

Read the cards.
Draw the bears.
Color the bears.
Write the words.

PURPOSE: To provide practice in reading and writing.

MATERIALS AND DIRECTIONS

Bear reading cards
Pencils
Crayons
Writing paper

Teacher provides Bear reading cards. Glue them on tag and laminate. If children are non-readers, you or a reader can read the card for them. The child can then draw the bears and write only the bear's name.

NOTE: The Panda looks like a black and white bear. It is probably related to the raccoon. This is a nice opportunity to share this information with your class.

Brown Bear

Most brown bears spend the winter in their dens. The rest of the year they like to play and eat. They like to catch fish to eat. They also like honey, berries and ants.

Polar Bear

Polar bears are some of the biggest and strongest animals in the world. They are very good swimmers. They use their front legs to paddle and their back legs to steer.

Giant Panda

Giant pandas live in China. Most pandas spend the whole day eating. Their favorite food is bamboo. Big pandas are good climbers.

Teddy Bear

Teddy bears are VERY special bears. They like to go everywhere with you. They really need a lot of hugs. When you are with them they understand and always love you no matter what you do.

LEARNING EXPERIENCE: Dress a Bear

TASK CARD

Dress a Bear
Cut out a bear.
Cut out bear clothes.
Glue clothes on bear.
Measure.

PURPOSE: To dress the bear and measure the bear clothes.

MATERIALS AND DIRECTIONS

Teacher runs bear on light brown paper. Run bear clothes on a variety of colors.

Scissors
Glue
Recording sheet
Pencils

Child cuts and dresses bear. Teacher provides a form of measurement—cm cubes or a non-standard tool such as paper clips.

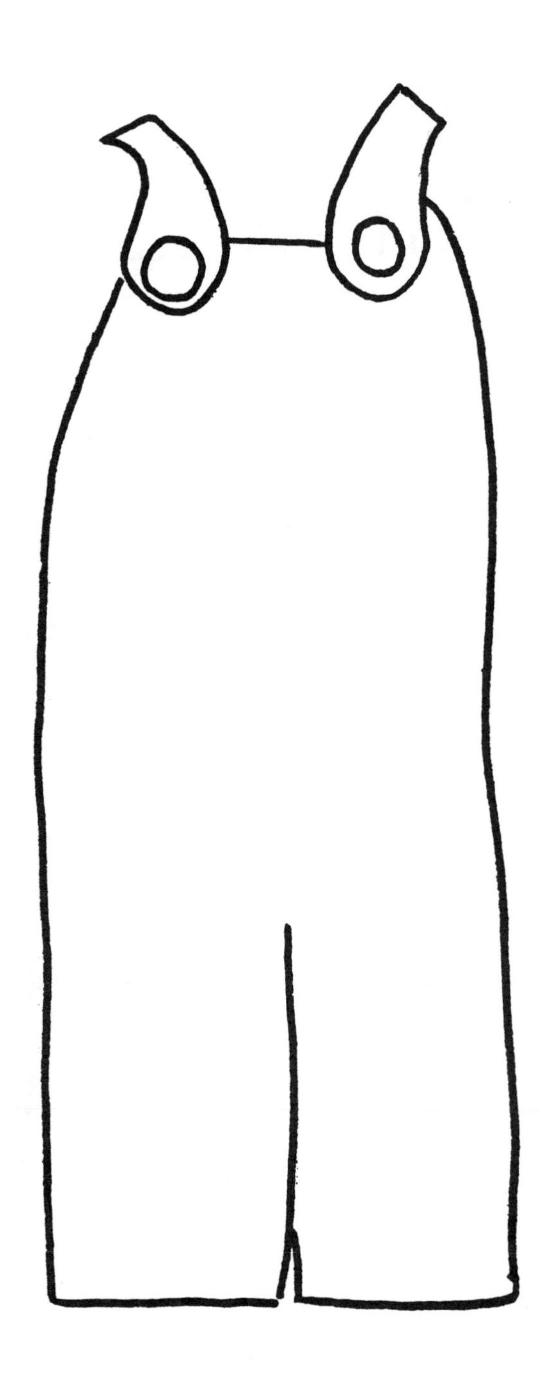

Measure the Bear

Name: ______________________________

Bear's arm ______________

Bear's leg ______________

Bear's head ______________

Bear's overalls __________

How tall is the bear? ____

What is your bears

name? ________________

LEARNING EXPERIENCE: Bear Words and Sentences

TASK CARD

Bear Words and Sentences

Use the word to write a sentence.

PURPOSE: To provide a sentence building experience using key words.

MATERIALS AND DIRECTIONS

Teacher makes several bear cards from pattern. Use words appropriate for your class. Run bear cards on colored paper, cut out and laminate.

Recording sheet
Pencils

Bear Words and Sentences

Name

Pattern for Bear Cards

LEARNING EXPERIENCE: Make a Dancing Bear

TASK CARD

Make a Dancing Bear

Cut out a tummy.
Cut out the other bear parts.
Color his face.
Use the brads to assemble.

PURPOSE: To cut and assemble a bear.

MATERIALS AND DIRECTIONS

Teacher provides bear parts run on light brown construction paper.
Provide tummy pattern and brown paper for tracing.

Brads
Crayons
Scissors

EXTENDED ACTIVITIES

* Child writes story about bear.
* Measure the bear parts and record.

LEARNING EXPERIENCE: How Many Blocks Balance the Bear?

TASK CARD

PURPOSE: To provide a balancing experience using non-standard measurement.

MATERIALS AND DIRECTIONS

Balance pans
Small blocks
Two small toy bears or other type stuffed animals
Recording sheet

Name ______________________

How many blocks balance the bear?

______ blocks = 1 bear

______ blocks = 2 bears

LEARNING EXPERIENCE: Bear Puzzle

TASK CARD

PURPOSE: To provide an experience in puzzle skills.

MATERIALS AND DIRECTIONS

Bear Puzzle
Crayons
Scissors
Glue
9" x 12" construction paper

Child cuts six pieces apart and reassembles them in the correct order on the sheet of construction paper.

LEARNING EXPERIENCE: Stuffed Animal Facts

TASK CARD

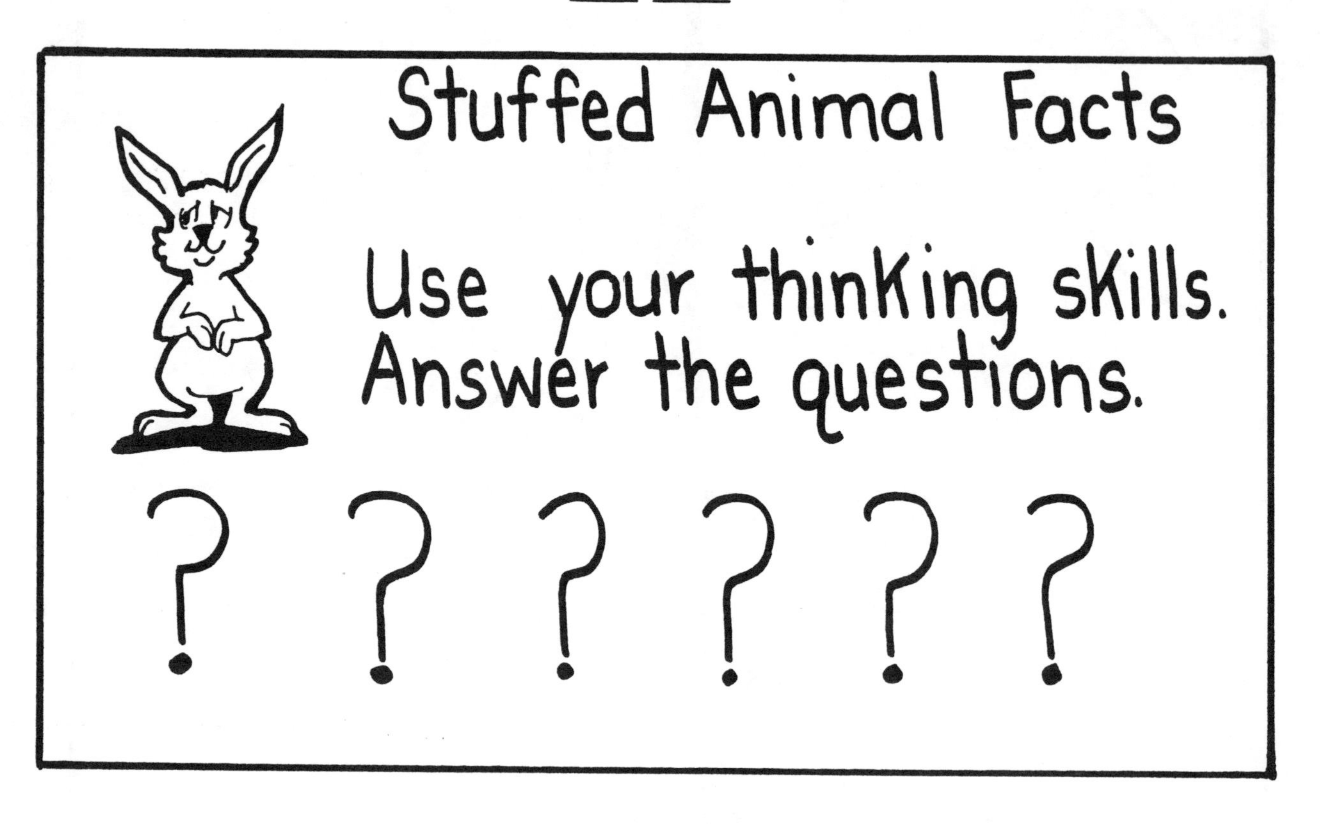

PURPOSE: To provide an experience in thinking and writing skills.

MATERIALS AND DIRECTIONS

Child's stuffed animal
Pencils
Recording sheet
Crayons

EXTENDED ACTIVITY

* Have children make a recording sheet about a friend's stuffed animal as well as on their own.

Stuffed Animal Facts

What color is your animal?

____

How tall is your animal?

____

How old is your animal?

____

How wide is your animal?

____

Turn your paper over and draw your stuffed animal.

LEARNING EXPERIENCE: My Stuffed Animal

TASK CARD

PURPOSE: To provide practice in completing sentences.

MATERIALS AND DIRECTIONS

Child's stuffed animal
Pencils
Crayons
Recording book

Teacher prepares a recording book for each child.

Name ______________________________

My Stuffed Animal

Complete the sentences.
Draw pictures.

This book is about ______________
my stuffed animal.

I got my stuffed animal when

____

____

In my house my stuffed animal lives

I talk to my stuffed animal about

My stuffed animal and I like to

One time my stuffed animal began to lose its stuffing and

LEARNING EXPERIENCE: What Size is Your Bear?

TASK CARD

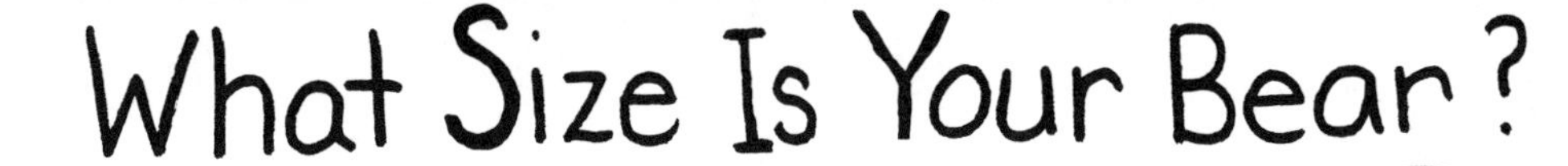

Draw your bear.
Color your bear.
Cut out your bear.
Glue your bear
on the bear chart.

Small Bear

Big Bear

PURPOSE: Sorting by size.

MATERIALS AND DIRECTIONS

Teacher prepares three large butcher paper charts. Label: 'Little', 'Medium', 'Big'. Construction paper, 4-1/2" x 6", for child to draw bear.

Crayons
Scissors
Glue

LEARNING EXPERIENCE: Porridge for Two Bears

PURPOSE: A cooking experience for 2 children to share; cooperation.

MATERIALS AND DIRECTIONS

Teacher provides ingredients in recipe. This recipe is for instant oatmeal packages.

Honey
Spoons and paper cups or bowls

EXTENDED ACTIVITIES

* We have also made a big batch of oatmeal and served all the children (and bears) at circle time. We let them add a spoon of raisins and honey. We add a little milk.

Porridge for Two Bears

$\frac{3}{4}$ cup hot water

1 package oatmeal

Stir.

Eat with 1 spoonful of

honey.

LEARNING EXPERIENCE: Bears Like to Eat

PURPOSE: A multi-sensory experience.

MATERIALS AND DIRECTIONS

Teacher provides appropriate food for children to taste, such as bread cubes, honey, peanut butter, tuna, berries, etc.

Bears like to eat...

Taste some bear food.
Record your favorite.

Bears like to eat...

Name ______________________________

I tasted ____________________
I tasted ____________________
I tasted ____________________
I tasted ____________________

My favorite bear food was ____________________

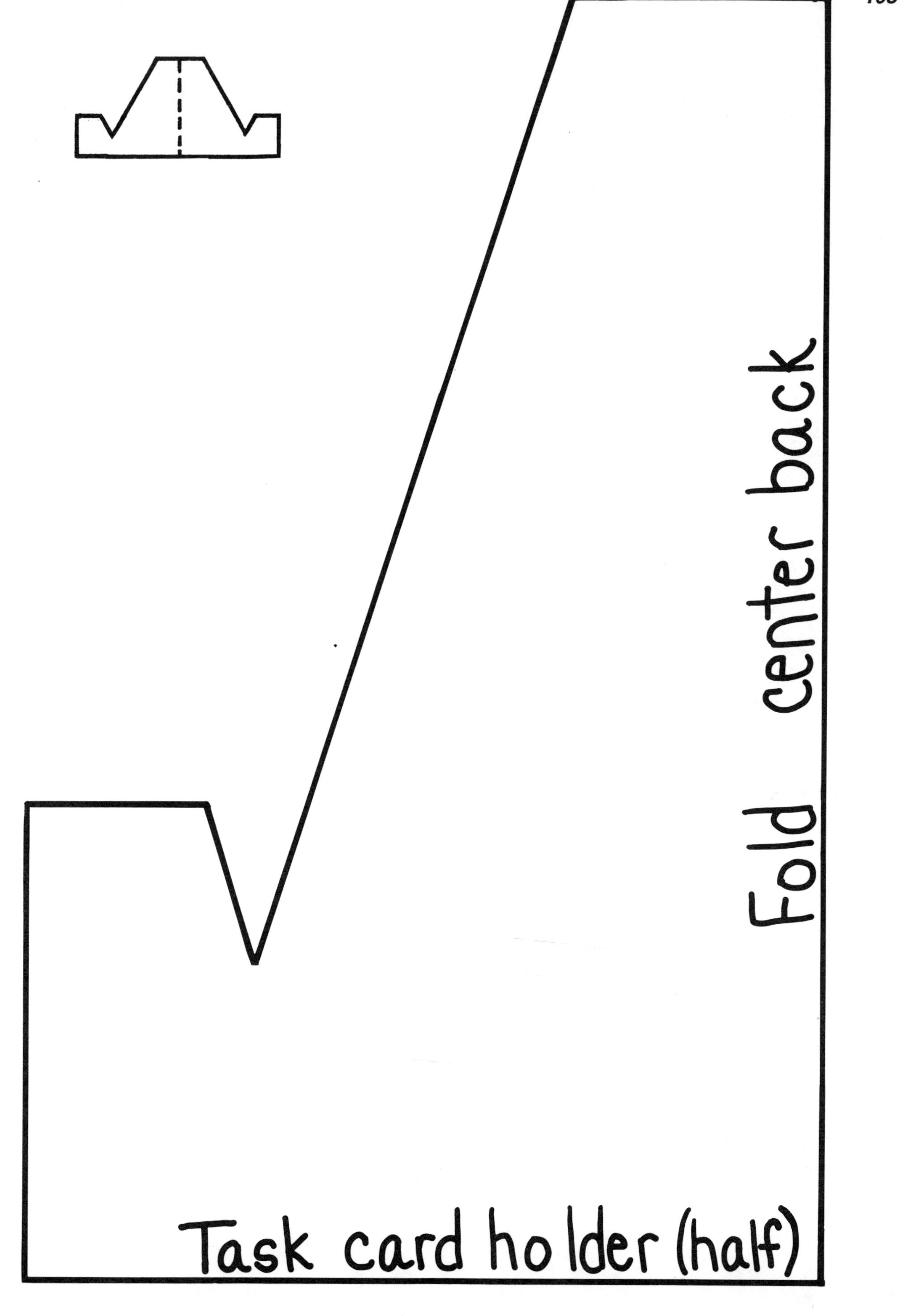
Fold center back
Task card holder (half)